# Monthly Profit Tracker

| Month | Total Spend | Total Sales | Total Profit |
|---|---|---|---|
|  |  |  |  |
|  |  |  |  |
|  |  |  |  |
|  |  |  |  |
|  |  |  |  |
|  |  |  |  |
|  |  |  |  |
|  |  |  |  |
|  |  |  |  |
|  |  |  |  |
|  |  |  |  |
|  |  |  |  |
|  |  |  |  |
|  |  |  |  |
|  |  |  |  |
|  |  |  |  |
|  |  |  |  |
|  |  |  |  |
|  |  |  |  |
|  |  |  |  |
|  |  |  |  |
|  |  |  |  |
|  |  |  |  |
|  |  |  |  |
|  |  |  |  |
|  |  |  |  |

# Purchase & Sales Tracker

DATES FROM _____

| Item | Purchase Date | Sale Date | Sale Website | Purchase Price | Sale Price | Profit |
|------|---------------|-----------|--------------|----------------|------------|--------|
| | | | | | | |
| | | | | | | |
| | | | | | | |
| | | | | | | |
| | | | | | | |
| | | | | | | |
| | | | | | | |
| | | | | | | |
| | | | | | | |
| | | | | | | |
| | | | | | | |
| | | | | | | |
| | | | | | | |
| | | | | | | |
| | | | | | | |
| | | | | | | |
| | | | | | | |
| | | | | | | |
| | | | | | | |
| | | | | | | |
| | | | | | | |
| | | | | | | |
| | | | | | | |
| | | | | | | |
| | | | | | | |
| | | | | | | |
| | | | | | | |

Total

# Purchase & Sales Tracker

DATES FROM _____

| Item | Purchase Date | Sale Date | Sale Website | Purchase Price | Sale Price | Profit |
|------|---------------|-----------|--------------|----------------|------------|--------|
|      |               |           |              |                |            |        |
|      |               |           |              |                |            |        |
|      |               |           |              |                |            |        |
|      |               |           |              |                |            |        |
|      |               |           |              |                |            |        |
|      |               |           |              |                |            |        |
|      |               |           |              |                |            |        |
|      |               |           |              |                |            |        |
|      |               |           |              |                |            |        |
|      |               |           |              |                |            |        |
|      |               |           |              |                |            |        |
|      |               |           |              |                |            |        |
|      |               |           |              |                |            |        |
|      |               |           |              |                |            |        |
|      |               |           |              |                |            |        |
|      |               |           |              |                |            |        |
|      |               |           |              |                |            |        |
|      |               |           |              |                |            |        |
|      |               |           |              |                |            |        |
|      |               |           |              |                |            |        |
|      |               |           |              |                |            |        |
|      |               |           |              |                |            |        |
|      |               |           |              |                |            |        |
|      |               |           |              |                |            |        |
|      |               |           |              |                |            |        |
|      |               |           |              |                |            |        |

Total

# Purchase & Sales Tracker

DATES FROM _____

| Item | Purchase Date | Sale Date | Sale Website | Purchase Price | Sale Price | Profit |
|------|---------------|-----------|--------------|----------------|------------|--------|
|  |  |  |  |  |  |  |
|  |  |  |  |  |  |  |
|  |  |  |  |  |  |  |
|  |  |  |  |  |  |  |
|  |  |  |  |  |  |  |
|  |  |  |  |  |  |  |
|  |  |  |  |  |  |  |
|  |  |  |  |  |  |  |
|  |  |  |  |  |  |  |
|  |  |  |  |  |  |  |
|  |  |  |  |  |  |  |
|  |  |  |  |  |  |  |
|  |  |  |  |  |  |  |
|  |  |  |  |  |  |  |
|  |  |  |  |  |  |  |
|  |  |  |  |  |  |  |
|  |  |  |  |  |  |  |
|  |  |  |  |  |  |  |
|  |  |  |  |  |  |  |
|  |  |  |  |  |  |  |
|  |  |  |  |  |  |  |
|  |  |  |  |  |  |  |
|  |  |  |  |  |  |  |
|  |  |  |  |  |  |  |
|  |  |  |  |  |  |  |
|  |  |  |  |  |  |  |
|  |  |  |  |  |  |  |

Total

# Purchase & Sales Tracker

DATES FROM _____

| Item | Purchase Date | Sale Date | Sale Website | Purchase Price | Sale Price | Profit |
|------|---------------|-----------|--------------|----------------|------------|--------|
|  |  |  |  |  |  |  |
|  |  |  |  |  |  |  |
|  |  |  |  |  |  |  |
|  |  |  |  |  |  |  |
|  |  |  |  |  |  |  |
|  |  |  |  |  |  |  |
|  |  |  |  |  |  |  |
|  |  |  |  |  |  |  |
|  |  |  |  |  |  |  |
|  |  |  |  |  |  |  |
|  |  |  |  |  |  |  |
|  |  |  |  |  |  |  |
|  |  |  |  |  |  |  |
|  |  |  |  |  |  |  |
|  |  |  |  |  |  |  |
|  |  |  |  |  |  |  |
|  |  |  |  |  |  |  |
|  |  |  |  |  |  |  |
|  |  |  |  |  |  |  |
|  |  |  |  |  |  |  |
|  |  |  |  |  |  |  |
|  |  |  |  |  |  |  |
|  |  |  |  |  |  |  |
|  |  |  |  |  |  |  |
|  |  |  |  |  |  |  |
|  |  |  |  |  |  |  |
|  |  |  |  |  |  |  |

Total | | | |

# Purchase & Sales Tracker

DATES FROM _____

| Item | Purchase Date | Sale Date | Sale Website | Purchase Price | Sale Price | Profit |
|---|---|---|---|---|---|---|
| | | | | | | |
| | | | | | | |
| | | | | | | |
| | | | | | | |
| | | | | | | |
| | | | | | | |
| | | | | | | |
| | | | | | | |
| | | | | | | |
| | | | | | | |
| | | | | | | |
| | | | | | | |
| | | | | | | |
| | | | | | | |
| | | | | | | |
| | | | | | | |
| | | | | | | |
| | | | | | | |
| | | | | | | |
| | | | | | | |
| | | | | | | |
| | | | | | | |
| | | | | | | |
| | | | | | | |
| | | | | | | |
| | | | | | | |
| | | | | | | |

Total

# Purchase & Sales Tracker

DATES FROM _____

| Item | Purchase Date | Sale Date | Sale Website | Purchase Price | Sale Price | Profit |
|---|---|---|---|---|---|---|
| | | | | | | |
| | | | | | | |
| | | | | | | |
| | | | | | | |
| | | | | | | |
| | | | | | | |
| | | | | | | |
| | | | | | | |
| | | | | | | |
| | | | | | | |
| | | | | | | |
| | | | | | | |
| | | | | | | |
| | | | | | | |
| | | | | | | |
| | | | | | | |
| | | | | | | |
| | | | | | | |
| | | | | | | |
| | | | | | | |
| | | | | | | |
| | | | | | | |
| | | | | | | |
| | | | | | | |
| | | | | | | |
| | | | | | | |

Total

# Purchase & Sales Tracker

DATES FROM _____

| Item | Purchase Date | Sale Date | Sale Website | Purchase Price | Sale Price | Profit |
|------|---------------|-----------|--------------|----------------|------------|--------|
|  |  |  |  |  |  |  |
|  |  |  |  |  |  |  |
|  |  |  |  |  |  |  |
|  |  |  |  |  |  |  |
|  |  |  |  |  |  |  |
|  |  |  |  |  |  |  |
|  |  |  |  |  |  |  |
|  |  |  |  |  |  |  |
|  |  |  |  |  |  |  |
|  |  |  |  |  |  |  |
|  |  |  |  |  |  |  |
|  |  |  |  |  |  |  |
|  |  |  |  |  |  |  |
|  |  |  |  |  |  |  |
|  |  |  |  |  |  |  |
|  |  |  |  |  |  |  |
|  |  |  |  |  |  |  |
|  |  |  |  |  |  |  |
|  |  |  |  |  |  |  |
|  |  |  |  |  |  |  |
|  |  |  |  |  |  |  |
|  |  |  |  |  |  |  |
|  |  |  |  |  |  |  |
|  |  |  |  |  |  |  |
|  |  |  |  |  |  |  |
|  |  |  |  |  |  |  |

Total

# Purchase & Sales Tracker

DATES FROM _____

| Item | Purchase Date | Sale Date | Sale Website | Purchase Price | Sale Price | Profit |
|------|---------------|-----------|--------------|----------------|------------|--------|
|  |  |  |  |  |  |  |
|  |  |  |  |  |  |  |
|  |  |  |  |  |  |  |
|  |  |  |  |  |  |  |
|  |  |  |  |  |  |  |
|  |  |  |  |  |  |  |
|  |  |  |  |  |  |  |
|  |  |  |  |  |  |  |
|  |  |  |  |  |  |  |
|  |  |  |  |  |  |  |
|  |  |  |  |  |  |  |
|  |  |  |  |  |  |  |
|  |  |  |  |  |  |  |
|  |  |  |  |  |  |  |
|  |  |  |  |  |  |  |
|  |  |  |  |  |  |  |
|  |  |  |  |  |  |  |
|  |  |  |  |  |  |  |
|  |  |  |  |  |  |  |
|  |  |  |  |  |  |  |
|  |  |  |  |  |  |  |
|  |  |  |  |  |  |  |
|  |  |  |  |  |  |  |
|  |  |  |  |  |  |  |
|  |  |  |  |  |  |  |
|  |  |  |  |  |  |  |

**Total**

# Purchase & Sales Tracker

DATES FROM _____

| Item | Purchase Date | Sale Date | Sale Website | Purchase Price | Sale Price | Profit |
|------|---------------|-----------|--------------|----------------|------------|--------|
|  |  |  |  |  |  |  |
|  |  |  |  |  |  |  |
|  |  |  |  |  |  |  |
|  |  |  |  |  |  |  |
|  |  |  |  |  |  |  |
|  |  |  |  |  |  |  |
|  |  |  |  |  |  |  |
|  |  |  |  |  |  |  |
|  |  |  |  |  |  |  |
|  |  |  |  |  |  |  |
|  |  |  |  |  |  |  |
|  |  |  |  |  |  |  |
|  |  |  |  |  |  |  |
|  |  |  |  |  |  |  |
|  |  |  |  |  |  |  |
|  |  |  |  |  |  |  |
|  |  |  |  |  |  |  |
|  |  |  |  |  |  |  |
|  |  |  |  |  |  |  |
|  |  |  |  |  |  |  |
|  |  |  |  |  |  |  |
|  |  |  |  |  |  |  |
|  |  |  |  |  |  |  |
|  |  |  |  |  |  |  |
|  |  |  |  |  |  |  |
|  |  |  |  |  |  |  |
|  |  |  |  |  |  |  |

Total

# Purchase & Sales Tracker

DATES FROM _____

| Item | Purchase Date | Sale Date | Sale Website | Purchase Price | Sale Price | Profit |
|------|------|------|------|------|------|------|
|  |  |  |  |  |  |  |
|  |  |  |  |  |  |  |
|  |  |  |  |  |  |  |
|  |  |  |  |  |  |  |
|  |  |  |  |  |  |  |
|  |  |  |  |  |  |  |
|  |  |  |  |  |  |  |
|  |  |  |  |  |  |  |
|  |  |  |  |  |  |  |
|  |  |  |  |  |  |  |
|  |  |  |  |  |  |  |
|  |  |  |  |  |  |  |
|  |  |  |  |  |  |  |
|  |  |  |  |  |  |  |
|  |  |  |  |  |  |  |
|  |  |  |  |  |  |  |
|  |  |  |  |  |  |  |
|  |  |  |  |  |  |  |
|  |  |  |  |  |  |  |
|  |  |  |  |  |  |  |
|  |  |  |  |  |  |  |
|  |  |  |  |  |  |  |
|  |  |  |  |  |  |  |
|  |  |  |  |  |  |  |
|  |  |  |  |  |  |  |
|  |  |  |  |  |  |  |
|  |  |  |  |  |  |  |
|  |  |  |  |  |  |  |
|  |  |  |  |  |  |  |

Total

# Purchase & Sales Tracker

DATES FROM _____

| Item | Purchase Date | Sale Date | Sale Website | Purchase Price | Sale Price | Profit |
|------|---------------|-----------|--------------|----------------|------------|--------|
| | | | | | | |
| | | | | | | |
| | | | | | | |
| | | | | | | |
| | | | | | | |
| | | | | | | |
| | | | | | | |
| | | | | | | |
| | | | | | | |
| | | | | | | |
| | | | | | | |
| | | | | | | |
| | | | | | | |
| | | | | | | |
| | | | | | | |
| | | | | | | |
| | | | | | | |
| | | | | | | |
| | | | | | | |
| | | | | | | |
| | | | | | | |
| | | | | | | |
| | | | | | | |
| | | | | | | |
| | | | | | | |
| | | | | | | |
| | | | | | | |
| | | | | | | |
| | | | | | | |

Total

# Purchase & Sales Tracker

DATES FROM _____

| Item | Purchase Date | Sale Date | Sale Website | Purchase Price | Sale Price | Profit |
|------|---------------|-----------|--------------|----------------|------------|--------|
|  |  |  |  |  |  |  |
|  |  |  |  |  |  |  |
|  |  |  |  |  |  |  |
|  |  |  |  |  |  |  |
|  |  |  |  |  |  |  |
|  |  |  |  |  |  |  |
|  |  |  |  |  |  |  |
|  |  |  |  |  |  |  |
|  |  |  |  |  |  |  |
|  |  |  |  |  |  |  |
|  |  |  |  |  |  |  |
|  |  |  |  |  |  |  |
|  |  |  |  |  |  |  |
|  |  |  |  |  |  |  |
|  |  |  |  |  |  |  |
|  |  |  |  |  |  |  |
|  |  |  |  |  |  |  |
|  |  |  |  |  |  |  |
|  |  |  |  |  |  |  |
|  |  |  |  |  |  |  |
|  |  |  |  |  |  |  |
|  |  |  |  |  |  |  |
|  |  |  |  |  |  |  |
|  |  |  |  |  |  |  |
|  |  |  |  |  |  |  |
|  |  |  |  |  |  |  |
|  |  |  |  |  |  |  |

Total

# Purchase & Sales Tracker

DATES FROM _____

| Item | Purchase Date | Sale Date | Sale Website | Purchase Price | Sale Price | Profit |
|---|---|---|---|---|---|---|
|  |  |  |  |  |  |  |
|  |  |  |  |  |  |  |
|  |  |  |  |  |  |  |
|  |  |  |  |  |  |  |
|  |  |  |  |  |  |  |
|  |  |  |  |  |  |  |
|  |  |  |  |  |  |  |
|  |  |  |  |  |  |  |
|  |  |  |  |  |  |  |
|  |  |  |  |  |  |  |
|  |  |  |  |  |  |  |
|  |  |  |  |  |  |  |
|  |  |  |  |  |  |  |
|  |  |  |  |  |  |  |
|  |  |  |  |  |  |  |
|  |  |  |  |  |  |  |
|  |  |  |  |  |  |  |
|  |  |  |  |  |  |  |
|  |  |  |  |  |  |  |
|  |  |  |  |  |  |  |
|  |  |  |  |  |  |  |
|  |  |  |  |  |  |  |
|  |  |  |  |  |  |  |
|  |  |  |  |  |  |  |
|  |  |  |  |  |  |  |
|  |  |  |  |  |  |  |
|  |  |  |  |  |  |  |
|  |  |  |  |  |  |  |

Total

# Purchase & Sales Tracker

DATES FROM _____

| Item | Purchase Date | Sale Date | Sale Website | Purchase Price | Sale Price | Profit |
|------|---------------|-----------|--------------|----------------|------------|--------|
|      |               |           |              |                |            |        |
|      |               |           |              |                |            |        |
|      |               |           |              |                |            |        |
|      |               |           |              |                |            |        |
|      |               |           |              |                |            |        |
|      |               |           |              |                |            |        |
|      |               |           |              |                |            |        |
|      |               |           |              |                |            |        |
|      |               |           |              |                |            |        |
|      |               |           |              |                |            |        |
|      |               |           |              |                |            |        |
|      |               |           |              |                |            |        |
|      |               |           |              |                |            |        |
|      |               |           |              |                |            |        |
|      |               |           |              |                |            |        |
|      |               |           |              |                |            |        |
|      |               |           |              |                |            |        |
|      |               |           |              |                |            |        |
|      |               |           |              |                |            |        |
|      |               |           |              |                |            |        |
|      |               |           |              |                |            |        |
|      |               |           |              |                |            |        |
|      |               |           |              |                |            |        |
|      |               |           |              |                |            |        |
|      |               |           |              |                |            |        |
|      |               |           |              |                |            |        |
|      |               |           |              |                |            |        |
|      |               |           |              |                |            |        |
|      |               |           |              |                |            |        |

Total | | |

# Purchase & Sales Tracker

DATES FROM _____

| Item | Purchase Date | Sale Date | Sale Website | Purchase Price | Sale Price | Profit |
|---|---|---|---|---|---|---|
|  |  |  |  |  |  |  |
|  |  |  |  |  |  |  |
|  |  |  |  |  |  |  |
|  |  |  |  |  |  |  |
|  |  |  |  |  |  |  |
|  |  |  |  |  |  |  |
|  |  |  |  |  |  |  |
|  |  |  |  |  |  |  |
|  |  |  |  |  |  |  |
|  |  |  |  |  |  |  |
|  |  |  |  |  |  |  |
|  |  |  |  |  |  |  |
|  |  |  |  |  |  |  |
|  |  |  |  |  |  |  |
|  |  |  |  |  |  |  |
|  |  |  |  |  |  |  |
|  |  |  |  |  |  |  |
|  |  |  |  |  |  |  |
|  |  |  |  |  |  |  |
|  |  |  |  |  |  |  |
|  |  |  |  |  |  |  |
|  |  |  |  |  |  |  |
|  |  |  |  |  |  |  |
|  |  |  |  |  |  |  |
|  |  |  |  |  |  |  |
|  |  |  |  |  |  |  |
|  |  |  |  |  |  |  |
|  |  |  |  |  |  |  |

Total

# Purchase & Sales Tracker

DATES FROM _____

| Item | Purchase Date | Sale Date | Sale Website | Purchase Price | Sale Price | Profit |
|------|---------------|-----------|--------------|----------------|------------|--------|
|  |  |  |  |  |  |  |
|  |  |  |  |  |  |  |
|  |  |  |  |  |  |  |
|  |  |  |  |  |  |  |
|  |  |  |  |  |  |  |
|  |  |  |  |  |  |  |
|  |  |  |  |  |  |  |
|  |  |  |  |  |  |  |
|  |  |  |  |  |  |  |
|  |  |  |  |  |  |  |
|  |  |  |  |  |  |  |
|  |  |  |  |  |  |  |
|  |  |  |  |  |  |  |
|  |  |  |  |  |  |  |
|  |  |  |  |  |  |  |
|  |  |  |  |  |  |  |
|  |  |  |  |  |  |  |
|  |  |  |  |  |  |  |
|  |  |  |  |  |  |  |
|  |  |  |  |  |  |  |
|  |  |  |  |  |  |  |
|  |  |  |  |  |  |  |
|  |  |  |  |  |  |  |
|  |  |  |  |  |  |  |
|  |  |  |  |  |  |  |
|  |  |  |  |  |  |  |

**Total**

# Purchase & Sales Tracker

DATES FROM _____

| Item | Purchase Date | Sale Date | Sale Website | Purchase Price | Sale Price | Profit |
|------|---------------|-----------|--------------|----------------|------------|--------|
|  |  |  |  |  |  |  |
|  |  |  |  |  |  |  |
|  |  |  |  |  |  |  |
|  |  |  |  |  |  |  |
|  |  |  |  |  |  |  |
|  |  |  |  |  |  |  |
|  |  |  |  |  |  |  |
|  |  |  |  |  |  |  |
|  |  |  |  |  |  |  |
|  |  |  |  |  |  |  |
|  |  |  |  |  |  |  |
|  |  |  |  |  |  |  |
|  |  |  |  |  |  |  |
|  |  |  |  |  |  |  |
|  |  |  |  |  |  |  |
|  |  |  |  |  |  |  |
|  |  |  |  |  |  |  |
|  |  |  |  |  |  |  |
|  |  |  |  |  |  |  |
|  |  |  |  |  |  |  |
|  |  |  |  |  |  |  |
|  |  |  |  |  |  |  |
|  |  |  |  |  |  |  |
|  |  |  |  |  |  |  |
|  |  |  |  |  |  |  |
|  |  |  |  |  |  |  |
|  |  |  |  |  |  |  |
|  |  |  |  |  |  |  |
|  |  |  |  |  |  |  |

Total

# Purchase & Sales Tracker

DATES FROM _____

| Item | Purchase Date | Sale Date | Sale Website | Purchase Price | Sale Price | Profit |
|------|---------------|-----------|--------------|----------------|------------|--------|
|      |               |           |              |                |            |        |
|      |               |           |              |                |            |        |
|      |               |           |              |                |            |        |
|      |               |           |              |                |            |        |
|      |               |           |              |                |            |        |
|      |               |           |              |                |            |        |
|      |               |           |              |                |            |        |
|      |               |           |              |                |            |        |
|      |               |           |              |                |            |        |
|      |               |           |              |                |            |        |
|      |               |           |              |                |            |        |
|      |               |           |              |                |            |        |
|      |               |           |              |                |            |        |
|      |               |           |              |                |            |        |
|      |               |           |              |                |            |        |
|      |               |           |              |                |            |        |
|      |               |           |              |                |            |        |
|      |               |           |              |                |            |        |
|      |               |           |              |                |            |        |
|      |               |           |              |                |            |        |
|      |               |           |              |                |            |        |
|      |               |           |              |                |            |        |
|      |               |           |              |                |            |        |
|      |               |           |              |                |            |        |
|      |               |           |              |                |            |        |
|      |               |           |              |                |            |        |

Total

# Purchase & Sales Tracker

**DATES FROM** _____

| Item | Purchase Date | Sale Date | Sale Website | Purchase Price | Sale Price | Profit |
|------|---------------|-----------|--------------|----------------|------------|--------|
| | | | | | | |
| | | | | | | |
| | | | | | | |
| | | | | | | |
| | | | | | | |
| | | | | | | |
| | | | | | | |
| | | | | | | |
| | | | | | | |
| | | | | | | |
| | | | | | | |
| | | | | | | |
| | | | | | | |
| | | | | | | |
| | | | | | | |
| | | | | | | |
| | | | | | | |
| | | | | | | |
| | | | | | | |
| | | | | | | |
| | | | | | | |
| | | | | | | |
| | | | | | | |
| | | | | | | |
| | | | | | | |
| | | | | | | |
| | | | | | | |
| | | | | | | |
| | | | | | | |

**Total** [ ] [ ] [ ]

# Purchase & Sales Tracker

DATES FROM _____

| Item | Purchase Date | Sale Date | Sale Website | Purchase Price | Sale Price | Profit |
|---|---|---|---|---|---|---|
|  |  |  |  |  |  |  |
|  |  |  |  |  |  |  |
|  |  |  |  |  |  |  |
|  |  |  |  |  |  |  |
|  |  |  |  |  |  |  |
|  |  |  |  |  |  |  |
|  |  |  |  |  |  |  |
|  |  |  |  |  |  |  |
|  |  |  |  |  |  |  |
|  |  |  |  |  |  |  |
|  |  |  |  |  |  |  |
|  |  |  |  |  |  |  |
|  |  |  |  |  |  |  |
|  |  |  |  |  |  |  |
|  |  |  |  |  |  |  |
|  |  |  |  |  |  |  |
|  |  |  |  |  |  |  |
|  |  |  |  |  |  |  |
|  |  |  |  |  |  |  |
|  |  |  |  |  |  |  |
|  |  |  |  |  |  |  |
|  |  |  |  |  |  |  |
|  |  |  |  |  |  |  |
|  |  |  |  |  |  |  |
|  |  |  |  |  |  |  |
|  |  |  |  |  |  |  |
|  |  |  |  |  |  |  |

Total

# Purchase & Sales Tracker

DATES FROM _____

| Item | Purchase Date | Sale Date | Sale Website | Purchase Price | Sale Price | Profit |
|------|---------------|-----------|--------------|----------------|------------|--------|
|      |               |           |              |                |            |        |
|      |               |           |              |                |            |        |
|      |               |           |              |                |            |        |
|      |               |           |              |                |            |        |
|      |               |           |              |                |            |        |
|      |               |           |              |                |            |        |
|      |               |           |              |                |            |        |
|      |               |           |              |                |            |        |
|      |               |           |              |                |            |        |
|      |               |           |              |                |            |        |
|      |               |           |              |                |            |        |
|      |               |           |              |                |            |        |
|      |               |           |              |                |            |        |
|      |               |           |              |                |            |        |
|      |               |           |              |                |            |        |
|      |               |           |              |                |            |        |
|      |               |           |              |                |            |        |
|      |               |           |              |                |            |        |
|      |               |           |              |                |            |        |
|      |               |           |              |                |            |        |
|      |               |           |              |                |            |        |
|      |               |           |              |                |            |        |
|      |               |           |              |                |            |        |
|      |               |           |              |                |            |        |
|      |               |           |              |                |            |        |
|      |               |           |              |                |            |        |
|      |               |           |              |                |            |        |

Total

# Purchase & Sales Tracker

DATES FROM _____

| Item | Purchase Date | Sale Date | Sale Website | Purchase Price | Sale Price | Profit |
|------|---------------|-----------|--------------|----------------|------------|--------|
|  |  |  |  |  |  |  |
|  |  |  |  |  |  |  |
|  |  |  |  |  |  |  |
|  |  |  |  |  |  |  |
|  |  |  |  |  |  |  |
|  |  |  |  |  |  |  |
|  |  |  |  |  |  |  |
|  |  |  |  |  |  |  |
|  |  |  |  |  |  |  |
|  |  |  |  |  |  |  |
|  |  |  |  |  |  |  |
|  |  |  |  |  |  |  |
|  |  |  |  |  |  |  |
|  |  |  |  |  |  |  |
|  |  |  |  |  |  |  |
|  |  |  |  |  |  |  |
|  |  |  |  |  |  |  |
|  |  |  |  |  |  |  |
|  |  |  |  |  |  |  |
|  |  |  |  |  |  |  |
|  |  |  |  |  |  |  |
|  |  |  |  |  |  |  |
|  |  |  |  |  |  |  |
|  |  |  |  |  |  |  |
|  |  |  |  |  |  |  |
|  |  |  |  |  |  |  |
|  |  |  |  |  |  |  |

Total

# Purchase & Sales Tracker

DATES FROM _____

| Item | Purchase Date | Sale Date | Sale Website | Purchase Price | Sale Price | Profit |
|------|---------------|-----------|--------------|----------------|------------|--------|
|  |  |  |  |  |  |  |
|  |  |  |  |  |  |  |
|  |  |  |  |  |  |  |
|  |  |  |  |  |  |  |
|  |  |  |  |  |  |  |
|  |  |  |  |  |  |  |
|  |  |  |  |  |  |  |
|  |  |  |  |  |  |  |
|  |  |  |  |  |  |  |
|  |  |  |  |  |  |  |
|  |  |  |  |  |  |  |
|  |  |  |  |  |  |  |
|  |  |  |  |  |  |  |
|  |  |  |  |  |  |  |
|  |  |  |  |  |  |  |
|  |  |  |  |  |  |  |
|  |  |  |  |  |  |  |
|  |  |  |  |  |  |  |
|  |  |  |  |  |  |  |
|  |  |  |  |  |  |  |
|  |  |  |  |  |  |  |
|  |  |  |  |  |  |  |
|  |  |  |  |  |  |  |
|  |  |  |  |  |  |  |
|  |  |  |  |  |  |  |
|  |  |  |  |  |  |  |
|  |  |  |  |  |  |  |

**Total**

# Purchase & Sales Tracker

DATES FROM _____

| Item | Purchase Date | Sale Date | Sale Website | Purchase Price | Sale Price | Profit |
|------|---------------|-----------|--------------|----------------|------------|--------|
|  |  |  |  |  |  |  |
|  |  |  |  |  |  |  |
|  |  |  |  |  |  |  |
|  |  |  |  |  |  |  |
|  |  |  |  |  |  |  |
|  |  |  |  |  |  |  |
|  |  |  |  |  |  |  |
|  |  |  |  |  |  |  |
|  |  |  |  |  |  |  |
|  |  |  |  |  |  |  |
|  |  |  |  |  |  |  |
|  |  |  |  |  |  |  |
|  |  |  |  |  |  |  |
|  |  |  |  |  |  |  |
|  |  |  |  |  |  |  |
|  |  |  |  |  |  |  |
|  |  |  |  |  |  |  |
|  |  |  |  |  |  |  |
|  |  |  |  |  |  |  |
|  |  |  |  |  |  |  |
|  |  |  |  |  |  |  |
|  |  |  |  |  |  |  |
|  |  |  |  |  |  |  |
|  |  |  |  |  |  |  |
|  |  |  |  |  |  |  |
|  |  |  |  |  |  |  |
|  |  |  |  |  |  |  |
|  |  |  |  |  |  |  |

Total | | | |

# Purchase & Sales Tracker

**DATES FROM** _____

| Item | Purchase Date | Sale Date | Sale Website | Purchase Price | Sale Price | Profit |
|---|---|---|---|---|---|---|
| | | | | | | |
| | | | | | | |
| | | | | | | |
| | | | | | | |
| | | | | | | |
| | | | | | | |
| | | | | | | |
| | | | | | | |
| | | | | | | |
| | | | | | | |
| | | | | | | |
| | | | | | | |
| | | | | | | |
| | | | | | | |
| | | | | | | |
| | | | | | | |
| | | | | | | |
| | | | | | | |
| | | | | | | |
| | | | | | | |
| | | | | | | |
| | | | | | | |
| | | | | | | |
| | | | | | | |
| | | | | | | |
| | | | | | | |
| | | | | | | |

**Total** | | | |

# Purchase & Sales Tracker

DATES FROM _____

| Item | Purchase Date | Sale Date | Sale Website | Purchase Price | Sale Price | Profit |
|------|---------------|-----------|--------------|----------------|------------|--------|
|      |               |           |              |                |            |        |
|      |               |           |              |                |            |        |
|      |               |           |              |                |            |        |
|      |               |           |              |                |            |        |
|      |               |           |              |                |            |        |
|      |               |           |              |                |            |        |
|      |               |           |              |                |            |        |
|      |               |           |              |                |            |        |
|      |               |           |              |                |            |        |
|      |               |           |              |                |            |        |
|      |               |           |              |                |            |        |
|      |               |           |              |                |            |        |
|      |               |           |              |                |            |        |
|      |               |           |              |                |            |        |
|      |               |           |              |                |            |        |
|      |               |           |              |                |            |        |
|      |               |           |              |                |            |        |
|      |               |           |              |                |            |        |
|      |               |           |              |                |            |        |
|      |               |           |              |                |            |        |
|      |               |           |              |                |            |        |
|      |               |           |              |                |            |        |
|      |               |           |              |                |            |        |
|      |               |           |              |                |            |        |
|      |               |           |              |                |            |        |
|      |               |           |              |                |            |        |
|      |               |           |              |                |            |        |

Total

# Purchase & Sales Tracker

DATES FROM _____

| Item | Purchase Date | Sale Date | Sale Website | Purchase Price | Sale Price | Profit |
|------|---------------|-----------|--------------|----------------|------------|--------|
|  |  |  |  |  |  |  |
|  |  |  |  |  |  |  |
|  |  |  |  |  |  |  |
|  |  |  |  |  |  |  |
|  |  |  |  |  |  |  |
|  |  |  |  |  |  |  |
|  |  |  |  |  |  |  |
|  |  |  |  |  |  |  |
|  |  |  |  |  |  |  |
|  |  |  |  |  |  |  |
|  |  |  |  |  |  |  |
|  |  |  |  |  |  |  |
|  |  |  |  |  |  |  |
|  |  |  |  |  |  |  |
|  |  |  |  |  |  |  |
|  |  |  |  |  |  |  |
|  |  |  |  |  |  |  |
|  |  |  |  |  |  |  |
|  |  |  |  |  |  |  |
|  |  |  |  |  |  |  |
|  |  |  |  |  |  |  |
|  |  |  |  |  |  |  |
|  |  |  |  |  |  |  |
|  |  |  |  |  |  |  |
|  |  |  |  |  |  |  |
|  |  |  |  |  |  |  |
|  |  |  |  |  |  |  |
|  |  |  |  |  |  |  |

Total

# Purchase & Sales Tracker

DATES FROM _____

| Item | Purchase Date | Sale Date | Sale Website | Purchase Price | Sale Price | Profit |
|---|---|---|---|---|---|---|
|  |  |  |  |  |  |  |
|  |  |  |  |  |  |  |
|  |  |  |  |  |  |  |
|  |  |  |  |  |  |  |
|  |  |  |  |  |  |  |
|  |  |  |  |  |  |  |
|  |  |  |  |  |  |  |
|  |  |  |  |  |  |  |
|  |  |  |  |  |  |  |
|  |  |  |  |  |  |  |
|  |  |  |  |  |  |  |
|  |  |  |  |  |  |  |
|  |  |  |  |  |  |  |
|  |  |  |  |  |  |  |
|  |  |  |  |  |  |  |
|  |  |  |  |  |  |  |
|  |  |  |  |  |  |  |
|  |  |  |  |  |  |  |
|  |  |  |  |  |  |  |
|  |  |  |  |  |  |  |
|  |  |  |  |  |  |  |
|  |  |  |  |  |  |  |
|  |  |  |  |  |  |  |
|  |  |  |  |  |  |  |
|  |  |  |  |  |  |  |
|  |  |  |  |  |  |  |

Total

# Purchase & Sales Tracker

DATES FROM _____

| Item | Purchase Date | Sale Date | Sale Website | Purchase Price | Sale Price | Profit |
|------|---------------|-----------|--------------|----------------|------------|--------|
|  |  |  |  |  |  |  |
|  |  |  |  |  |  |  |
|  |  |  |  |  |  |  |
|  |  |  |  |  |  |  |
|  |  |  |  |  |  |  |
|  |  |  |  |  |  |  |
|  |  |  |  |  |  |  |
|  |  |  |  |  |  |  |
|  |  |  |  |  |  |  |
|  |  |  |  |  |  |  |
|  |  |  |  |  |  |  |
|  |  |  |  |  |  |  |
|  |  |  |  |  |  |  |
|  |  |  |  |  |  |  |
|  |  |  |  |  |  |  |
|  |  |  |  |  |  |  |
|  |  |  |  |  |  |  |
|  |  |  |  |  |  |  |
|  |  |  |  |  |  |  |
|  |  |  |  |  |  |  |
|  |  |  |  |  |  |  |
|  |  |  |  |  |  |  |
|  |  |  |  |  |  |  |
|  |  |  |  |  |  |  |
|  |  |  |  |  |  |  |
|  |  |  |  |  |  |  |
|  |  |  |  |  |  |  |

Total

# Purchase & Sales Tracker

DATES FROM _____

| Item | Purchase Date | Sale Date | Sale Website | Purchase Price | Sale Price | Profit |
|------|---------------|-----------|--------------|----------------|------------|--------|
|  |  |  |  |  |  |  |
|  |  |  |  |  |  |  |
|  |  |  |  |  |  |  |
|  |  |  |  |  |  |  |
|  |  |  |  |  |  |  |
|  |  |  |  |  |  |  |
|  |  |  |  |  |  |  |
|  |  |  |  |  |  |  |
|  |  |  |  |  |  |  |
|  |  |  |  |  |  |  |
|  |  |  |  |  |  |  |
|  |  |  |  |  |  |  |
|  |  |  |  |  |  |  |
|  |  |  |  |  |  |  |
|  |  |  |  |  |  |  |
|  |  |  |  |  |  |  |
|  |  |  |  |  |  |  |
|  |  |  |  |  |  |  |
|  |  |  |  |  |  |  |
|  |  |  |  |  |  |  |
|  |  |  |  |  |  |  |
|  |  |  |  |  |  |  |
|  |  |  |  |  |  |  |
|  |  |  |  |  |  |  |
|  |  |  |  |  |  |  |
|  |  |  |  |  |  |  |
|  |  |  |  |  |  |  |

Total

# Purchase & Sales Tracker

DATES FROM _____

| Item | Purchase Date | Sale Date | Sale Website | Purchase Price | Sale Price | Profit |
|------|------|------|------|------|------|------|
| | | | | | | |
| | | | | | | |
| | | | | | | |
| | | | | | | |
| | | | | | | |
| | | | | | | |
| | | | | | | |
| | | | | | | |
| | | | | | | |
| | | | | | | |
| | | | | | | |
| | | | | | | |
| | | | | | | |
| | | | | | | |
| | | | | | | |
| | | | | | | |
| | | | | | | |
| | | | | | | |
| | | | | | | |
| | | | | | | |
| | | | | | | |
| | | | | | | |
| | | | | | | |
| | | | | | | |
| | | | | | | |
| | | | | | | |
| | | | | | | |

Total

# Purchase & Sales Tracker

DATES FROM _____

| Item | Purchase Date | Sale Date | Sale Website | Purchase Price | Sale Price | Profit |
|------|---------------|-----------|--------------|----------------|------------|--------|
|      |               |           |              |                |            |        |
|      |               |           |              |                |            |        |
|      |               |           |              |                |            |        |
|      |               |           |              |                |            |        |
|      |               |           |              |                |            |        |
|      |               |           |              |                |            |        |
|      |               |           |              |                |            |        |
|      |               |           |              |                |            |        |
|      |               |           |              |                |            |        |
|      |               |           |              |                |            |        |
|      |               |           |              |                |            |        |
|      |               |           |              |                |            |        |
|      |               |           |              |                |            |        |
|      |               |           |              |                |            |        |
|      |               |           |              |                |            |        |
|      |               |           |              |                |            |        |
|      |               |           |              |                |            |        |
|      |               |           |              |                |            |        |
|      |               |           |              |                |            |        |
|      |               |           |              |                |            |        |
|      |               |           |              |                |            |        |
|      |               |           |              |                |            |        |
|      |               |           |              |                |            |        |
|      |               |           |              |                |            |        |
|      |               |           |              |                |            |        |
|      |               |           |              |                |            |        |

**Total**

# Purchase & Sales Tracker

DATES FROM _____

| Item | Purchase Date | Sale Date | Sale Website | Purchase Price | Sale Price | Profit |
|------|---------------|-----------|--------------|----------------|------------|--------|
|  |  |  |  |  |  |  |
|  |  |  |  |  |  |  |
|  |  |  |  |  |  |  |
|  |  |  |  |  |  |  |
|  |  |  |  |  |  |  |
|  |  |  |  |  |  |  |
|  |  |  |  |  |  |  |
|  |  |  |  |  |  |  |
|  |  |  |  |  |  |  |
|  |  |  |  |  |  |  |
|  |  |  |  |  |  |  |
|  |  |  |  |  |  |  |
|  |  |  |  |  |  |  |
|  |  |  |  |  |  |  |
|  |  |  |  |  |  |  |
|  |  |  |  |  |  |  |
|  |  |  |  |  |  |  |
|  |  |  |  |  |  |  |
|  |  |  |  |  |  |  |
|  |  |  |  |  |  |  |
|  |  |  |  |  |  |  |
|  |  |  |  |  |  |  |
|  |  |  |  |  |  |  |
|  |  |  |  |  |  |  |
|  |  |  |  |  |  |  |
|  |  |  |  |  |  |  |

Total

# Purchase & Sales Tracker

DATES FROM _____

| Item | Purchase Date | Sale Date | Sale Website | Purchase Price | Sale Price | Profit |
|------|---------------|-----------|--------------|----------------|------------|--------|
|      |               |           |              |                |            |        |
|      |               |           |              |                |            |        |
|      |               |           |              |                |            |        |
|      |               |           |              |                |            |        |
|      |               |           |              |                |            |        |
|      |               |           |              |                |            |        |
|      |               |           |              |                |            |        |
|      |               |           |              |                |            |        |
|      |               |           |              |                |            |        |
|      |               |           |              |                |            |        |
|      |               |           |              |                |            |        |
|      |               |           |              |                |            |        |
|      |               |           |              |                |            |        |
|      |               |           |              |                |            |        |
|      |               |           |              |                |            |        |
|      |               |           |              |                |            |        |
|      |               |           |              |                |            |        |
|      |               |           |              |                |            |        |
|      |               |           |              |                |            |        |
|      |               |           |              |                |            |        |
|      |               |           |              |                |            |        |
|      |               |           |              |                |            |        |
|      |               |           |              |                |            |        |
|      |               |           |              |                |            |        |
|      |               |           |              |                |            |        |
|      |               |           |              |                |            |        |
|      |               |           |              |                |            |        |

Total

# Purchase & Sales Tracker

DATES FROM _____

| Item | Purchase Date | Sale Date | Sale Website | Purchase Price | Sale Price | Profit |
|------|---------------|-----------|--------------|----------------|------------|--------|
|  |  |  |  |  |  |  |
|  |  |  |  |  |  |  |
|  |  |  |  |  |  |  |
|  |  |  |  |  |  |  |
|  |  |  |  |  |  |  |
|  |  |  |  |  |  |  |
|  |  |  |  |  |  |  |
|  |  |  |  |  |  |  |
|  |  |  |  |  |  |  |
|  |  |  |  |  |  |  |
|  |  |  |  |  |  |  |
|  |  |  |  |  |  |  |
|  |  |  |  |  |  |  |
|  |  |  |  |  |  |  |
|  |  |  |  |  |  |  |
|  |  |  |  |  |  |  |
|  |  |  |  |  |  |  |
|  |  |  |  |  |  |  |
|  |  |  |  |  |  |  |
|  |  |  |  |  |  |  |
|  |  |  |  |  |  |  |
|  |  |  |  |  |  |  |
|  |  |  |  |  |  |  |
|  |  |  |  |  |  |  |
|  |  |  |  |  |  |  |
|  |  |  |  |  |  |  |
|  |  |  |  |  |  |  |
|  |  |  |  |  |  |  |

Total

# Purchase & Sales Tracker

DATES FROM _____

| Item | Purchase Date | Sale Date | Sale Website | Purchase Price | Sale Price | Profit |
|---|---|---|---|---|---|---|
|  |  |  |  |  |  |  |
|  |  |  |  |  |  |  |
|  |  |  |  |  |  |  |
|  |  |  |  |  |  |  |
|  |  |  |  |  |  |  |
|  |  |  |  |  |  |  |
|  |  |  |  |  |  |  |
|  |  |  |  |  |  |  |
|  |  |  |  |  |  |  |
|  |  |  |  |  |  |  |
|  |  |  |  |  |  |  |
|  |  |  |  |  |  |  |
|  |  |  |  |  |  |  |
|  |  |  |  |  |  |  |
|  |  |  |  |  |  |  |
|  |  |  |  |  |  |  |
|  |  |  |  |  |  |  |
|  |  |  |  |  |  |  |
|  |  |  |  |  |  |  |
|  |  |  |  |  |  |  |
|  |  |  |  |  |  |  |
|  |  |  |  |  |  |  |
|  |  |  |  |  |  |  |
|  |  |  |  |  |  |  |
|  |  |  |  |  |  |  |
|  |  |  |  |  |  |  |
|  |  |  |  |  |  |  |
|  |  |  |  |  |  |  |

**Total** [        |        |        ]

# Purchase & Sales Tracker

DATES FROM _____

| Item | Purchase Date | Sale Date | Sale Website | Purchase Price | Sale Price | Profit |
|------|--------------|-----------|--------------|----------------|------------|--------|
|  |  |  |  |  |  |  |
|  |  |  |  |  |  |  |
|  |  |  |  |  |  |  |
|  |  |  |  |  |  |  |
|  |  |  |  |  |  |  |
|  |  |  |  |  |  |  |
|  |  |  |  |  |  |  |
|  |  |  |  |  |  |  |
|  |  |  |  |  |  |  |
|  |  |  |  |  |  |  |
|  |  |  |  |  |  |  |
|  |  |  |  |  |  |  |
|  |  |  |  |  |  |  |
|  |  |  |  |  |  |  |
|  |  |  |  |  |  |  |
|  |  |  |  |  |  |  |
|  |  |  |  |  |  |  |
|  |  |  |  |  |  |  |
|  |  |  |  |  |  |  |
|  |  |  |  |  |  |  |
|  |  |  |  |  |  |  |
|  |  |  |  |  |  |  |
|  |  |  |  |  |  |  |
|  |  |  |  |  |  |  |
|  |  |  |  |  |  |  |
|  |  |  |  |  |  |  |
|  |  |  |  |  |  |  |
|  |  |  |  |  |  |  |

Total

# Purchase & Sales Tracker

DATES FROM _____

| Item | Purchase Date | Sale Date | Sale Website | Purchase Price | Sale Price | Profit |
|---|---|---|---|---|---|---|
| | | | | | | |
| | | | | | | |
| | | | | | | |
| | | | | | | |
| | | | | | | |
| | | | | | | |
| | | | | | | |
| | | | | | | |
| | | | | | | |
| | | | | | | |
| | | | | | | |
| | | | | | | |
| | | | | | | |
| | | | | | | |
| | | | | | | |
| | | | | | | |
| | | | | | | |
| | | | | | | |
| | | | | | | |
| | | | | | | |
| | | | | | | |
| | | | | | | |
| | | | | | | |
| | | | | | | |
| | | | | | | |
| | | | | | | |
| | | | | | | |
| | | | | | | |

Total [   ] [   ] [   ]

# Purchase & Sales Tracker

DATES FROM _____

| Item | Purchase Date | Sale Date | Sale Website | Purchase Price | Sale Price | Profit |
|------|---------------|-----------|--------------|----------------|------------|--------|
|      |               |           |              |                |            |        |
|      |               |           |              |                |            |        |
|      |               |           |              |                |            |        |
|      |               |           |              |                |            |        |
|      |               |           |              |                |            |        |
|      |               |           |              |                |            |        |
|      |               |           |              |                |            |        |
|      |               |           |              |                |            |        |
|      |               |           |              |                |            |        |
|      |               |           |              |                |            |        |
|      |               |           |              |                |            |        |
|      |               |           |              |                |            |        |
|      |               |           |              |                |            |        |
|      |               |           |              |                |            |        |
|      |               |           |              |                |            |        |
|      |               |           |              |                |            |        |
|      |               |           |              |                |            |        |
|      |               |           |              |                |            |        |
|      |               |           |              |                |            |        |
|      |               |           |              |                |            |        |
|      |               |           |              |                |            |        |
|      |               |           |              |                |            |        |
|      |               |           |              |                |            |        |
|      |               |           |              |                |            |        |
|      |               |           |              |                |            |        |
|      |               |           |              |                |            |        |
|      |               |           |              |                |            |        |

Total [ ] [ ] [ ]

# Purchase & Sales Tracker

DATES FROM _____

| Item | Purchase Date | Sale Date | Sale Website | Purchase Price | Sale Price | Profit |
|------|---------------|-----------|--------------|----------------|------------|--------|
|  |  |  |  |  |  |  |
|  |  |  |  |  |  |  |
|  |  |  |  |  |  |  |
|  |  |  |  |  |  |  |
|  |  |  |  |  |  |  |
|  |  |  |  |  |  |  |
|  |  |  |  |  |  |  |
|  |  |  |  |  |  |  |
|  |  |  |  |  |  |  |
|  |  |  |  |  |  |  |
|  |  |  |  |  |  |  |
|  |  |  |  |  |  |  |
|  |  |  |  |  |  |  |
|  |  |  |  |  |  |  |
|  |  |  |  |  |  |  |
|  |  |  |  |  |  |  |
|  |  |  |  |  |  |  |
|  |  |  |  |  |  |  |
|  |  |  |  |  |  |  |
|  |  |  |  |  |  |  |
|  |  |  |  |  |  |  |
|  |  |  |  |  |  |  |
|  |  |  |  |  |  |  |
|  |  |  |  |  |  |  |
|  |  |  |  |  |  |  |
|  |  |  |  |  |  |  |

Total

# Purchase & Sales Tracker

**DATES FROM** _____

| Item | Purchase Date | Sale Date | Sale Website | Purchase Price | Sale Price | Profit |
|------|---------------|-----------|--------------|----------------|------------|--------|
|  |  |  |  |  |  |  |
|  |  |  |  |  |  |  |
|  |  |  |  |  |  |  |
|  |  |  |  |  |  |  |
|  |  |  |  |  |  |  |
|  |  |  |  |  |  |  |
|  |  |  |  |  |  |  |
|  |  |  |  |  |  |  |
|  |  |  |  |  |  |  |
|  |  |  |  |  |  |  |
|  |  |  |  |  |  |  |
|  |  |  |  |  |  |  |
|  |  |  |  |  |  |  |
|  |  |  |  |  |  |  |
|  |  |  |  |  |  |  |
|  |  |  |  |  |  |  |
|  |  |  |  |  |  |  |
|  |  |  |  |  |  |  |
|  |  |  |  |  |  |  |
|  |  |  |  |  |  |  |
|  |  |  |  |  |  |  |
|  |  |  |  |  |  |  |
|  |  |  |  |  |  |  |
|  |  |  |  |  |  |  |
|  |  |  |  |  |  |  |
|  |  |  |  |  |  |  |
|  |  |  |  |  |  |  |

**Total**

# Purchase & Sales Tracker

DATES FROM _____

| Item | Purchase Date | Sale Date | Sale Website | Purchase Price | Sale Price | Profit |
|------|---------------|-----------|--------------|----------------|------------|--------|
|      |               |           |              |                |            |        |
|      |               |           |              |                |            |        |
|      |               |           |              |                |            |        |
|      |               |           |              |                |            |        |
|      |               |           |              |                |            |        |
|      |               |           |              |                |            |        |
|      |               |           |              |                |            |        |
|      |               |           |              |                |            |        |
|      |               |           |              |                |            |        |
|      |               |           |              |                |            |        |
|      |               |           |              |                |            |        |
|      |               |           |              |                |            |        |
|      |               |           |              |                |            |        |
|      |               |           |              |                |            |        |
|      |               |           |              |                |            |        |
|      |               |           |              |                |            |        |
|      |               |           |              |                |            |        |
|      |               |           |              |                |            |        |
|      |               |           |              |                |            |        |
|      |               |           |              |                |            |        |
|      |               |           |              |                |            |        |
|      |               |           |              |                |            |        |
|      |               |           |              |                |            |        |
|      |               |           |              |                |            |        |
|      |               |           |              |                |            |        |
|      |               |           |              |                |            |        |
|      |               |           |              |                |            |        |

Total

# Purchase & Sales Tracker

DATES FROM _____

| Item | Purchase Date | Sale Date | Sale Website | Purchase Price | Sale Price | Profit |
|------|--------------|-----------|--------------|----------------|------------|--------|
|      |              |           |              |                |            |        |
|      |              |           |              |                |            |        |
|      |              |           |              |                |            |        |
|      |              |           |              |                |            |        |
|      |              |           |              |                |            |        |
|      |              |           |              |                |            |        |
|      |              |           |              |                |            |        |
|      |              |           |              |                |            |        |
|      |              |           |              |                |            |        |
|      |              |           |              |                |            |        |
|      |              |           |              |                |            |        |
|      |              |           |              |                |            |        |
|      |              |           |              |                |            |        |
|      |              |           |              |                |            |        |
|      |              |           |              |                |            |        |
|      |              |           |              |                |            |        |
|      |              |           |              |                |            |        |
|      |              |           |              |                |            |        |
|      |              |           |              |                |            |        |
|      |              |           |              |                |            |        |
|      |              |           |              |                |            |        |
|      |              |           |              |                |            |        |
|      |              |           |              |                |            |        |
|      |              |           |              |                |            |        |
|      |              |           |              |                |            |        |
|      |              |           |              |                |            |        |
|      |              |           |              |                |            |        |

Total

# Purchase & Sales Tracker

DATES FROM _____

| Item | Purchase Date | Sale Date | Sale Website | Purchase Price | Sale Price | Profit |
|------|---------------|-----------|--------------|----------------|------------|--------|
|      |               |           |              |                |            |        |
|      |               |           |              |                |            |        |
|      |               |           |              |                |            |        |
|      |               |           |              |                |            |        |
|      |               |           |              |                |            |        |
|      |               |           |              |                |            |        |
|      |               |           |              |                |            |        |
|      |               |           |              |                |            |        |
|      |               |           |              |                |            |        |
|      |               |           |              |                |            |        |
|      |               |           |              |                |            |        |
|      |               |           |              |                |            |        |
|      |               |           |              |                |            |        |
|      |               |           |              |                |            |        |
|      |               |           |              |                |            |        |
|      |               |           |              |                |            |        |
|      |               |           |              |                |            |        |
|      |               |           |              |                |            |        |
|      |               |           |              |                |            |        |
|      |               |           |              |                |            |        |
|      |               |           |              |                |            |        |
|      |               |           |              |                |            |        |
|      |               |           |              |                |            |        |
|      |               |           |              |                |            |        |
|      |               |           |              |                |            |        |
|      |               |           |              |                |            |        |
|      |               |           |              |                |            |        |

**Total**

# Purchase & Sales Tracker

DATES FROM _____

| Item | Purchase Date | Sale Date | Sale Website | Purchase Price | Sale Price | Profit |
|------|---------------|-----------|--------------|----------------|------------|--------|
|      |               |           |              |                |            |        |
|      |               |           |              |                |            |        |
|      |               |           |              |                |            |        |
|      |               |           |              |                |            |        |
|      |               |           |              |                |            |        |
|      |               |           |              |                |            |        |
|      |               |           |              |                |            |        |
|      |               |           |              |                |            |        |
|      |               |           |              |                |            |        |
|      |               |           |              |                |            |        |
|      |               |           |              |                |            |        |
|      |               |           |              |                |            |        |
|      |               |           |              |                |            |        |
|      |               |           |              |                |            |        |
|      |               |           |              |                |            |        |
|      |               |           |              |                |            |        |
|      |               |           |              |                |            |        |
|      |               |           |              |                |            |        |
|      |               |           |              |                |            |        |
|      |               |           |              |                |            |        |
|      |               |           |              |                |            |        |
|      |               |           |              |                |            |        |
|      |               |           |              |                |            |        |
|      |               |           |              |                |            |        |
|      |               |           |              |                |            |        |
|      |               |           |              |                |            |        |
|      |               |           |              |                |            |        |
|      |               |           |              |                |            |        |

Total

# Purchase & Sales Tracker

DATES FROM _____

| Item | Purchase Date | Sale Date | Sale Website | Purchase Price | Sale Price | Profit |
|---|---|---|---|---|---|---|
| | | | | | | |
| | | | | | | |
| | | | | | | |
| | | | | | | |
| | | | | | | |
| | | | | | | |
| | | | | | | |
| | | | | | | |
| | | | | | | |
| | | | | | | |
| | | | | | | |
| | | | | | | |
| | | | | | | |
| | | | | | | |
| | | | | | | |
| | | | | | | |
| | | | | | | |
| | | | | | | |
| | | | | | | |
| | | | | | | |
| | | | | | | |
| | | | | | | |
| | | | | | | |
| | | | | | | |
| | | | | | | |
| | | | | | | |

Total

# Purchase & Sales Tracker

DATES FROM _____

| Item | Purchase Date | Sale Date | Sale Website | Purchase Price | Sale Price | Profit |
|------|---------------|-----------|--------------|----------------|------------|--------|
| | | | | | | |
| | | | | | | |
| | | | | | | |
| | | | | | | |
| | | | | | | |
| | | | | | | |
| | | | | | | |
| | | | | | | |
| | | | | | | |
| | | | | | | |
| | | | | | | |
| | | | | | | |
| | | | | | | |
| | | | | | | |
| | | | | | | |
| | | | | | | |
| | | | | | | |
| | | | | | | |
| | | | | | | |
| | | | | | | |
| | | | | | | |
| | | | | | | |
| | | | | | | |
| | | | | | | |
| | | | | | | |
| | | | | | | |
| | | | | | | |
| | | | | | | |

Total

# Purchase & Sales Tracker

DATES FROM _____

| Item | Purchase Date | Sale Date | Sale Website | Purchase Price | Sale Price | Profit |
|---|---|---|---|---|---|---|
| | | | | | | |
| | | | | | | |
| | | | | | | |
| | | | | | | |
| | | | | | | |
| | | | | | | |
| | | | | | | |
| | | | | | | |
| | | | | | | |
| | | | | | | |
| | | | | | | |
| | | | | | | |
| | | | | | | |
| | | | | | | |
| | | | | | | |
| | | | | | | |
| | | | | | | |
| | | | | | | |
| | | | | | | |
| | | | | | | |
| | | | | | | |
| | | | | | | |
| | | | | | | |
| | | | | | | |
| | | | | | | |
| | | | | | | |
| | | | | | | |
| | | | | | | |

Total

# Purchase & Sales Tracker

DATES FROM _____

| Item | Purchase Date | Sale Date | Sale Website | Purchase Price | Sale Price | Profit |
|------|---------------|-----------|--------------|----------------|------------|--------|
| | | | | | | |
| | | | | | | |
| | | | | | | |
| | | | | | | |
| | | | | | | |
| | | | | | | |
| | | | | | | |
| | | | | | | |
| | | | | | | |
| | | | | | | |
| | | | | | | |
| | | | | | | |
| | | | | | | |
| | | | | | | |
| | | | | | | |
| | | | | | | |
| | | | | | | |
| | | | | | | |
| | | | | | | |
| | | | | | | |
| | | | | | | |
| | | | | | | |
| | | | | | | |
| | | | | | | |
| | | | | | | |
| | | | | | | |
| | | | | | | |

Total | | | |

# Purchase & Sales Tracker

DATES FROM _____

| Item | Purchase Date | Sale Date | Sale Website | Purchase Price | Sale Price | Profit |
|------|---------------|-----------|--------------|----------------|------------|--------|
|  |  |  |  |  |  |  |
|  |  |  |  |  |  |  |
|  |  |  |  |  |  |  |
|  |  |  |  |  |  |  |
|  |  |  |  |  |  |  |
|  |  |  |  |  |  |  |
|  |  |  |  |  |  |  |
|  |  |  |  |  |  |  |
|  |  |  |  |  |  |  |
|  |  |  |  |  |  |  |
|  |  |  |  |  |  |  |
|  |  |  |  |  |  |  |
|  |  |  |  |  |  |  |
|  |  |  |  |  |  |  |
|  |  |  |  |  |  |  |
|  |  |  |  |  |  |  |
|  |  |  |  |  |  |  |
|  |  |  |  |  |  |  |
|  |  |  |  |  |  |  |
|  |  |  |  |  |  |  |
|  |  |  |  |  |  |  |
|  |  |  |  |  |  |  |
|  |  |  |  |  |  |  |
|  |  |  |  |  |  |  |
|  |  |  |  |  |  |  |
|  |  |  |  |  |  |  |
|  |  |  |  |  |  |  |

Total

# Purchase & Sales Tracker

DATES FROM _____

| Item | Purchase Date | Sale Date | Sale Website | Purchase Price | Sale Price | Profit |
|------|---------------|-----------|--------------|----------------|------------|--------|
|      |               |           |              |                |            |        |
|      |               |           |              |                |            |        |
|      |               |           |              |                |            |        |
|      |               |           |              |                |            |        |
|      |               |           |              |                |            |        |
|      |               |           |              |                |            |        |
|      |               |           |              |                |            |        |
|      |               |           |              |                |            |        |
|      |               |           |              |                |            |        |
|      |               |           |              |                |            |        |
|      |               |           |              |                |            |        |
|      |               |           |              |                |            |        |
|      |               |           |              |                |            |        |
|      |               |           |              |                |            |        |
|      |               |           |              |                |            |        |
|      |               |           |              |                |            |        |
|      |               |           |              |                |            |        |
|      |               |           |              |                |            |        |
|      |               |           |              |                |            |        |
|      |               |           |              |                |            |        |
|      |               |           |              |                |            |        |
|      |               |           |              |                |            |        |
|      |               |           |              |                |            |        |
|      |               |           |              |                |            |        |
|      |               |           |              |                |            |        |
|      |               |           |              |                |            |        |

Total

# Purchase & Sales Tracker

DATES FROM _____

| Item | Purchase Date | Sale Date | Sale Website | Purchase Price | Sale Price | Profit |
|------|---------------|-----------|--------------|----------------|------------|--------|
|      |               |           |              |                |            |        |
|      |               |           |              |                |            |        |
|      |               |           |              |                |            |        |
|      |               |           |              |                |            |        |
|      |               |           |              |                |            |        |
|      |               |           |              |                |            |        |
|      |               |           |              |                |            |        |
|      |               |           |              |                |            |        |
|      |               |           |              |                |            |        |
|      |               |           |              |                |            |        |
|      |               |           |              |                |            |        |
|      |               |           |              |                |            |        |
|      |               |           |              |                |            |        |
|      |               |           |              |                |            |        |
|      |               |           |              |                |            |        |
|      |               |           |              |                |            |        |
|      |               |           |              |                |            |        |
|      |               |           |              |                |            |        |
|      |               |           |              |                |            |        |
|      |               |           |              |                |            |        |
|      |               |           |              |                |            |        |
|      |               |           |              |                |            |        |
|      |               |           |              |                |            |        |
|      |               |           |              |                |            |        |
|      |               |           |              |                |            |        |
|      |               |           |              |                |            |        |
|      |               |           |              |                |            |        |

Total

# Purchase & Sales Tracker

DATES FROM _____

| Item | Purchase Date | Sale Date | Sale Website | Purchase Price | Sale Price | Profit |
|------|---------------|-----------|--------------|----------------|------------|--------|
| | | | | | | |
| | | | | | | |
| | | | | | | |
| | | | | | | |
| | | | | | | |
| | | | | | | |
| | | | | | | |
| | | | | | | |
| | | | | | | |
| | | | | | | |
| | | | | | | |
| | | | | | | |
| | | | | | | |
| | | | | | | |
| | | | | | | |
| | | | | | | |
| | | | | | | |
| | | | | | | |
| | | | | | | |
| | | | | | | |
| | | | | | | |
| | | | | | | |
| | | | | | | |
| | | | | | | |
| | | | | | | |
| | | | | | | |

Total | | |

# Purchase & Sales Tracker

DATES FROM _____

| Item | Purchase Date | Sale Date | Sale Website | Purchase Price | Sale Price | Profit |
|------|---------------|-----------|--------------|----------------|------------|--------|
|      |               |           |              |                |            |        |
|      |               |           |              |                |            |        |
|      |               |           |              |                |            |        |
|      |               |           |              |                |            |        |
|      |               |           |              |                |            |        |
|      |               |           |              |                |            |        |
|      |               |           |              |                |            |        |
|      |               |           |              |                |            |        |
|      |               |           |              |                |            |        |
|      |               |           |              |                |            |        |
|      |               |           |              |                |            |        |
|      |               |           |              |                |            |        |
|      |               |           |              |                |            |        |
|      |               |           |              |                |            |        |
|      |               |           |              |                |            |        |
|      |               |           |              |                |            |        |
|      |               |           |              |                |            |        |
|      |               |           |              |                |            |        |
|      |               |           |              |                |            |        |
|      |               |           |              |                |            |        |
|      |               |           |              |                |            |        |
|      |               |           |              |                |            |        |
|      |               |           |              |                |            |        |
|      |               |           |              |                |            |        |
|      |               |           |              |                |            |        |
|      |               |           |              |                |            |        |

Total

# Purchase & Sales Tracker

DATES FROM _____

| Item | Purchase Date | Sale Date | Sale Website | Purchase Price | Sale Price | Profit |
|------|--------------|-----------|--------------|----------------|------------|--------|
|  |  |  |  |  |  |  |
|  |  |  |  |  |  |  |
|  |  |  |  |  |  |  |
|  |  |  |  |  |  |  |
|  |  |  |  |  |  |  |
|  |  |  |  |  |  |  |
|  |  |  |  |  |  |  |
|  |  |  |  |  |  |  |
|  |  |  |  |  |  |  |
|  |  |  |  |  |  |  |
|  |  |  |  |  |  |  |
|  |  |  |  |  |  |  |
|  |  |  |  |  |  |  |
|  |  |  |  |  |  |  |
|  |  |  |  |  |  |  |
|  |  |  |  |  |  |  |
|  |  |  |  |  |  |  |
|  |  |  |  |  |  |  |
|  |  |  |  |  |  |  |
|  |  |  |  |  |  |  |
|  |  |  |  |  |  |  |
|  |  |  |  |  |  |  |
|  |  |  |  |  |  |  |
|  |  |  |  |  |  |  |
|  |  |  |  |  |  |  |
|  |  |  |  |  |  |  |
|  |  |  |  |  |  |  |
|  |  |  |  |  |  |  |

Total

# Purchase & Sales Tracker

DATES FROM _____

| Item | Purchase Date | Sale Date | Sale Website | Purchase Price | Sale Price | Profit |
|------|---------------|-----------|--------------|----------------|------------|--------|
|  |  |  |  |  |  |  |
|  |  |  |  |  |  |  |
|  |  |  |  |  |  |  |
|  |  |  |  |  |  |  |
|  |  |  |  |  |  |  |
|  |  |  |  |  |  |  |
|  |  |  |  |  |  |  |
|  |  |  |  |  |  |  |
|  |  |  |  |  |  |  |
|  |  |  |  |  |  |  |
|  |  |  |  |  |  |  |
|  |  |  |  |  |  |  |
|  |  |  |  |  |  |  |
|  |  |  |  |  |  |  |
|  |  |  |  |  |  |  |
|  |  |  |  |  |  |  |
|  |  |  |  |  |  |  |
|  |  |  |  |  |  |  |
|  |  |  |  |  |  |  |
|  |  |  |  |  |  |  |
|  |  |  |  |  |  |  |
|  |  |  |  |  |  |  |
|  |  |  |  |  |  |  |
|  |  |  |  |  |  |  |
|  |  |  |  |  |  |  |
|  |  |  |  |  |  |  |
|  |  |  |  |  |  |  |

**Total** _____

# Purchase & Sales Tracker

DATES FROM _____

| Item | Purchase Date | Sale Date | Sale Website | Purchase Price | Sale Price | Profit |
|------|--------------|-----------|--------------|----------------|------------|--------|
|      |              |           |              |                |            |        |
|      |              |           |              |                |            |        |
|      |              |           |              |                |            |        |
|      |              |           |              |                |            |        |
|      |              |           |              |                |            |        |
|      |              |           |              |                |            |        |
|      |              |           |              |                |            |        |
|      |              |           |              |                |            |        |
|      |              |           |              |                |            |        |
|      |              |           |              |                |            |        |
|      |              |           |              |                |            |        |
|      |              |           |              |                |            |        |
|      |              |           |              |                |            |        |
|      |              |           |              |                |            |        |
|      |              |           |              |                |            |        |
|      |              |           |              |                |            |        |
|      |              |           |              |                |            |        |
|      |              |           |              |                |            |        |
|      |              |           |              |                |            |        |
|      |              |           |              |                |            |        |
|      |              |           |              |                |            |        |
|      |              |           |              |                |            |        |
|      |              |           |              |                |            |        |
|      |              |           |              |                |            |        |
|      |              |           |              |                |            |        |
|      |              |           |              |                |            |        |

Total

# Purchase & Sales Tracker

DATES FROM _____

| Item | Purchase Date | Sale Date | Sale Website | Purchase Price | Sale Price | Profit |
|------|---------------|-----------|--------------|----------------|------------|--------|
|      |               |           |              |                |            |        |
|      |               |           |              |                |            |        |
|      |               |           |              |                |            |        |
|      |               |           |              |                |            |        |
|      |               |           |              |                |            |        |
|      |               |           |              |                |            |        |
|      |               |           |              |                |            |        |
|      |               |           |              |                |            |        |
|      |               |           |              |                |            |        |
|      |               |           |              |                |            |        |
|      |               |           |              |                |            |        |
|      |               |           |              |                |            |        |
|      |               |           |              |                |            |        |
|      |               |           |              |                |            |        |
|      |               |           |              |                |            |        |
|      |               |           |              |                |            |        |
|      |               |           |              |                |            |        |
|      |               |           |              |                |            |        |
|      |               |           |              |                |            |        |
|      |               |           |              |                |            |        |
|      |               |           |              |                |            |        |
|      |               |           |              |                |            |        |
|      |               |           |              |                |            |        |
|      |               |           |              |                |            |        |
|      |               |           |              |                |            |        |
|      |               |           |              |                |            |        |

Total

# Purchase & Sales Tracker

DATES FROM _____

| Item | Purchase Date | Sale Date | Sale Website | Purchase Price | Sale Price | Profit |
|------|---------------|-----------|--------------|----------------|------------|--------|
|      |               |           |              |                |            |        |
|      |               |           |              |                |            |        |
|      |               |           |              |                |            |        |
|      |               |           |              |                |            |        |
|      |               |           |              |                |            |        |
|      |               |           |              |                |            |        |
|      |               |           |              |                |            |        |
|      |               |           |              |                |            |        |
|      |               |           |              |                |            |        |
|      |               |           |              |                |            |        |
|      |               |           |              |                |            |        |
|      |               |           |              |                |            |        |
|      |               |           |              |                |            |        |
|      |               |           |              |                |            |        |
|      |               |           |              |                |            |        |
|      |               |           |              |                |            |        |
|      |               |           |              |                |            |        |
|      |               |           |              |                |            |        |
|      |               |           |              |                |            |        |
|      |               |           |              |                |            |        |
|      |               |           |              |                |            |        |
|      |               |           |              |                |            |        |
|      |               |           |              |                |            |        |
|      |               |           |              |                |            |        |
|      |               |           |              |                |            |        |
|      |               |           |              |                |            |        |
|      |               |           |              |                |            |        |
|      |               |           |              |                |            |        |

Total

# Purchase & Sales Tracker

DATES FROM _____

| Item | Purchase Date | Sale Date | Sale Website | Purchase Price | Sale Price | Profit |
|------|---------------|-----------|--------------|----------------|------------|--------|
|  |  |  |  |  |  |  |
|  |  |  |  |  |  |  |
|  |  |  |  |  |  |  |
|  |  |  |  |  |  |  |
|  |  |  |  |  |  |  |
|  |  |  |  |  |  |  |
|  |  |  |  |  |  |  |
|  |  |  |  |  |  |  |
|  |  |  |  |  |  |  |
|  |  |  |  |  |  |  |
|  |  |  |  |  |  |  |
|  |  |  |  |  |  |  |
|  |  |  |  |  |  |  |
|  |  |  |  |  |  |  |
|  |  |  |  |  |  |  |
|  |  |  |  |  |  |  |
|  |  |  |  |  |  |  |
|  |  |  |  |  |  |  |
|  |  |  |  |  |  |  |
|  |  |  |  |  |  |  |
|  |  |  |  |  |  |  |
|  |  |  |  |  |  |  |
|  |  |  |  |  |  |  |
|  |  |  |  |  |  |  |
|  |  |  |  |  |  |  |
|  |  |  |  |  |  |  |
|  |  |  |  |  |  |  |
|  |  |  |  |  |  |  |

**Total** [____] [____] [____]

# Purchase & Sales Tracker

DATES FROM _____

| Item | Purchase Date | Sale Date | Sale Website | Purchase Price | Sale Price | Profit |
|------|---------------|-----------|--------------|----------------|------------|--------|
|      |               |           |              |                |            |        |
|      |               |           |              |                |            |        |
|      |               |           |              |                |            |        |
|      |               |           |              |                |            |        |
|      |               |           |              |                |            |        |
|      |               |           |              |                |            |        |
|      |               |           |              |                |            |        |
|      |               |           |              |                |            |        |
|      |               |           |              |                |            |        |
|      |               |           |              |                |            |        |
|      |               |           |              |                |            |        |
|      |               |           |              |                |            |        |
|      |               |           |              |                |            |        |
|      |               |           |              |                |            |        |
|      |               |           |              |                |            |        |
|      |               |           |              |                |            |        |
|      |               |           |              |                |            |        |
|      |               |           |              |                |            |        |
|      |               |           |              |                |            |        |
|      |               |           |              |                |            |        |
|      |               |           |              |                |            |        |
|      |               |           |              |                |            |        |
|      |               |           |              |                |            |        |
|      |               |           |              |                |            |        |
|      |               |           |              |                |            |        |
|      |               |           |              |                |            |        |
|      |               |           |              |                |            |        |

Total

# Purchase & Sales Tracker

DATES FROM _____

| Item | Purchase Date | Sale Date | Sale Website | Purchase Price | Sale Price | Profit |
|---|---|---|---|---|---|---|
| | | | | | | |
| | | | | | | |
| | | | | | | |
| | | | | | | |
| | | | | | | |
| | | | | | | |
| | | | | | | |
| | | | | | | |
| | | | | | | |
| | | | | | | |
| | | | | | | |
| | | | | | | |
| | | | | | | |
| | | | | | | |
| | | | | | | |
| | | | | | | |
| | | | | | | |
| | | | | | | |
| | | | | | | |
| | | | | | | |
| | | | | | | |
| | | | | | | |
| | | | | | | |
| | | | | | | |
| | | | | | | |
| | | | | | | |
| | | | | | | |
| | | | | | | |

Total _____

# Purchase & Sales Tracker

DATES FROM _____

| Item | Purchase Date | Sale Date | Sale Website | Purchase Price | Sale Price | Profit |
|------|---------------|-----------|--------------|----------------|------------|--------|
| | | | | | | |
| | | | | | | |
| | | | | | | |
| | | | | | | |
| | | | | | | |
| | | | | | | |
| | | | | | | |
| | | | | | | |
| | | | | | | |
| | | | | | | |
| | | | | | | |
| | | | | | | |
| | | | | | | |
| | | | | | | |
| | | | | | | |
| | | | | | | |
| | | | | | | |
| | | | | | | |
| | | | | | | |
| | | | | | | |
| | | | | | | |
| | | | | | | |
| | | | | | | |
| | | | | | | |
| | | | | | | |
| | | | | | | |
| | | | | | | |
| | | | | | | |
| | | | | | | |

Total

# Purchase & Sales Tracker

DATES FROM _____

| Item | Purchase Date | Sale Date | Sale Website | Purchase Price | Sale Price | Profit |
|------|---------------|-----------|--------------|----------------|------------|--------|
|      |               |           |              |                |            |        |
|      |               |           |              |                |            |        |
|      |               |           |              |                |            |        |
|      |               |           |              |                |            |        |
|      |               |           |              |                |            |        |
|      |               |           |              |                |            |        |
|      |               |           |              |                |            |        |
|      |               |           |              |                |            |        |
|      |               |           |              |                |            |        |
|      |               |           |              |                |            |        |
|      |               |           |              |                |            |        |
|      |               |           |              |                |            |        |
|      |               |           |              |                |            |        |
|      |               |           |              |                |            |        |
|      |               |           |              |                |            |        |
|      |               |           |              |                |            |        |
|      |               |           |              |                |            |        |
|      |               |           |              |                |            |        |
|      |               |           |              |                |            |        |
|      |               |           |              |                |            |        |
|      |               |           |              |                |            |        |
|      |               |           |              |                |            |        |
|      |               |           |              |                |            |        |
|      |               |           |              |                |            |        |
|      |               |           |              |                |            |        |
|      |               |           |              |                |            |        |

**Total**

# Purchase & Sales Tracker

DATES FROM _____

| Item | Purchase Date | Sale Date | Sale Website | Purchase Price | Sale Price | Profit |
|------|---------------|-----------|--------------|----------------|------------|--------|
|  |  |  |  |  |  |  |
|  |  |  |  |  |  |  |
|  |  |  |  |  |  |  |
|  |  |  |  |  |  |  |
|  |  |  |  |  |  |  |
|  |  |  |  |  |  |  |
|  |  |  |  |  |  |  |
|  |  |  |  |  |  |  |
|  |  |  |  |  |  |  |
|  |  |  |  |  |  |  |
|  |  |  |  |  |  |  |
|  |  |  |  |  |  |  |
|  |  |  |  |  |  |  |
|  |  |  |  |  |  |  |
|  |  |  |  |  |  |  |
|  |  |  |  |  |  |  |
|  |  |  |  |  |  |  |
|  |  |  |  |  |  |  |
|  |  |  |  |  |  |  |
|  |  |  |  |  |  |  |
|  |  |  |  |  |  |  |
|  |  |  |  |  |  |  |
|  |  |  |  |  |  |  |
|  |  |  |  |  |  |  |
|  |  |  |  |  |  |  |
|  |  |  |  |  |  |  |
|  |  |  |  |  |  |  |

Total

# Purchase & Sales Tracker

DATES FROM _____

| Item | Purchase Date | Sale Date | Sale Website | Purchase Price | Sale Price | Profit |
|------|---------------|-----------|--------------|----------------|------------|--------|
|      |               |           |              |                |            |        |
|      |               |           |              |                |            |        |
|      |               |           |              |                |            |        |
|      |               |           |              |                |            |        |
|      |               |           |              |                |            |        |
|      |               |           |              |                |            |        |
|      |               |           |              |                |            |        |
|      |               |           |              |                |            |        |
|      |               |           |              |                |            |        |
|      |               |           |              |                |            |        |
|      |               |           |              |                |            |        |
|      |               |           |              |                |            |        |
|      |               |           |              |                |            |        |
|      |               |           |              |                |            |        |
|      |               |           |              |                |            |        |
|      |               |           |              |                |            |        |
|      |               |           |              |                |            |        |
|      |               |           |              |                |            |        |
|      |               |           |              |                |            |        |
|      |               |           |              |                |            |        |
|      |               |           |              |                |            |        |
|      |               |           |              |                |            |        |
|      |               |           |              |                |            |        |
|      |               |           |              |                |            |        |
|      |               |           |              |                |            |        |
|      |               |           |              |                |            |        |
|      |               |           |              |                |            |        |

Total

# Purchase & Sales Tracker

DATES FROM _____

| Item | Purchase Date | Sale Date | Sale Website | Purchase Price | Sale Price | Profit |
|------|---------------|-----------|--------------|----------------|------------|--------|
| | | | | | | |
| | | | | | | |
| | | | | | | |
| | | | | | | |
| | | | | | | |
| | | | | | | |
| | | | | | | |
| | | | | | | |
| | | | | | | |
| | | | | | | |
| | | | | | | |
| | | | | | | |
| | | | | | | |
| | | | | | | |
| | | | | | | |
| | | | | | | |
| | | | | | | |
| | | | | | | |
| | | | | | | |
| | | | | | | |
| | | | | | | |
| | | | | | | |
| | | | | | | |
| | | | | | | |
| | | | | | | |
| | | | | | | |

**Total**

# Purchase & Sales Tracker

DATES FROM _____

| Item | Purchase Date | Sale Date | Sale Website | Purchase Price | Sale Price | Profit |
|---|---|---|---|---|---|---|
|  |  |  |  |  |  |  |
|  |  |  |  |  |  |  |
|  |  |  |  |  |  |  |
|  |  |  |  |  |  |  |
|  |  |  |  |  |  |  |
|  |  |  |  |  |  |  |
|  |  |  |  |  |  |  |
|  |  |  |  |  |  |  |
|  |  |  |  |  |  |  |
|  |  |  |  |  |  |  |
|  |  |  |  |  |  |  |
|  |  |  |  |  |  |  |
|  |  |  |  |  |  |  |
|  |  |  |  |  |  |  |
|  |  |  |  |  |  |  |
|  |  |  |  |  |  |  |
|  |  |  |  |  |  |  |
|  |  |  |  |  |  |  |
|  |  |  |  |  |  |  |
|  |  |  |  |  |  |  |
|  |  |  |  |  |  |  |
|  |  |  |  |  |  |  |
|  |  |  |  |  |  |  |
|  |  |  |  |  |  |  |
|  |  |  |  |  |  |  |
|  |  |  |  |  |  |  |
|  |  |  |  |  |  |  |
|  |  |  |  |  |  |  |

Total

# Purchase & Sales Tracker

DATES FROM _____

| Item | Purchase Date | Sale Date | Sale Website | Purchase Price | Sale Price | Profit |
|------|---------------|-----------|--------------|----------------|------------|--------|
| | | | | | | |
| | | | | | | |
| | | | | | | |
| | | | | | | |
| | | | | | | |
| | | | | | | |
| | | | | | | |
| | | | | | | |
| | | | | | | |
| | | | | | | |
| | | | | | | |
| | | | | | | |
| | | | | | | |
| | | | | | | |
| | | | | | | |
| | | | | | | |
| | | | | | | |
| | | | | | | |
| | | | | | | |
| | | | | | | |
| | | | | | | |
| | | | | | | |
| | | | | | | |
| | | | | | | |
| | | | | | | |
| | | | | | | |
| | | | | | | |

Total

# Purchase & Sales Tracker

DATES FROM _____

| Item | Purchase Date | Sale Date | Sale Website | Purchase Price | Sale Price | Profit |
|------|---------------|-----------|--------------|----------------|------------|--------|
|      |               |           |              |                |            |        |
|      |               |           |              |                |            |        |
|      |               |           |              |                |            |        |
|      |               |           |              |                |            |        |
|      |               |           |              |                |            |        |
|      |               |           |              |                |            |        |
|      |               |           |              |                |            |        |
|      |               |           |              |                |            |        |
|      |               |           |              |                |            |        |
|      |               |           |              |                |            |        |
|      |               |           |              |                |            |        |
|      |               |           |              |                |            |        |
|      |               |           |              |                |            |        |
|      |               |           |              |                |            |        |
|      |               |           |              |                |            |        |
|      |               |           |              |                |            |        |
|      |               |           |              |                |            |        |
|      |               |           |              |                |            |        |
|      |               |           |              |                |            |        |
|      |               |           |              |                |            |        |
|      |               |           |              |                |            |        |
|      |               |           |              |                |            |        |
|      |               |           |              |                |            |        |
|      |               |           |              |                |            |        |
|      |               |           |              |                |            |        |
|      |               |           |              |                |            |        |
|      |               |           |              |                |            |        |

Total

# Purchase & Sales Tracker

DATES FROM _____

| Item | Purchase Date | Sale Date | Sale Website | Purchase Price | Sale Price | Profit |
|------|---------------|-----------|--------------|----------------|------------|--------|
| | | | | | | |
| | | | | | | |
| | | | | | | |
| | | | | | | |
| | | | | | | |
| | | | | | | |
| | | | | | | |
| | | | | | | |
| | | | | | | |
| | | | | | | |
| | | | | | | |
| | | | | | | |
| | | | | | | |
| | | | | | | |
| | | | | | | |
| | | | | | | |
| | | | | | | |
| | | | | | | |
| | | | | | | |
| | | | | | | |
| | | | | | | |
| | | | | | | |
| | | | | | | |
| | | | | | | |
| | | | | | | |
| | | | | | | |

Total | | |

# Purchase & Sales Tracker

DATES FROM _____

| Item | Purchase Date | Sale Date | Sale Website | Purchase Price | Sale Price | Profit |
|------|---------------|-----------|--------------|----------------|------------|--------|
|  |  |  |  |  |  |  |
|  |  |  |  |  |  |  |
|  |  |  |  |  |  |  |
|  |  |  |  |  |  |  |
|  |  |  |  |  |  |  |
|  |  |  |  |  |  |  |
|  |  |  |  |  |  |  |
|  |  |  |  |  |  |  |
|  |  |  |  |  |  |  |
|  |  |  |  |  |  |  |
|  |  |  |  |  |  |  |
|  |  |  |  |  |  |  |
|  |  |  |  |  |  |  |
|  |  |  |  |  |  |  |
|  |  |  |  |  |  |  |
|  |  |  |  |  |  |  |
|  |  |  |  |  |  |  |
|  |  |  |  |  |  |  |
|  |  |  |  |  |  |  |
|  |  |  |  |  |  |  |
|  |  |  |  |  |  |  |
|  |  |  |  |  |  |  |
|  |  |  |  |  |  |  |
|  |  |  |  |  |  |  |
|  |  |  |  |  |  |  |
|  |  |  |  |  |  |  |
|  |  |  |  |  |  |  |

Total

# Purchase & Sales Tracker

DATES FROM _____

| Item | Purchase Date | Sale Date | Sale Website | Purchase Price | Sale Price | Profit |
|---|---|---|---|---|---|---|
| | | | | | | |
| | | | | | | |
| | | | | | | |
| | | | | | | |
| | | | | | | |
| | | | | | | |
| | | | | | | |
| | | | | | | |
| | | | | | | |
| | | | | | | |
| | | | | | | |
| | | | | | | |
| | | | | | | |
| | | | | | | |
| | | | | | | |
| | | | | | | |
| | | | | | | |
| | | | | | | |
| | | | | | | |
| | | | | | | |
| | | | | | | |
| | | | | | | |
| | | | | | | |
| | | | | | | |
| | | | | | | |
| | | | | | | |
| | | | | | | |
| | | | | | | |

Total

# Purchase & Sales Tracker

DATES FROM _____

| Item | Purchase Date | Sale Date | Sale Website | Purchase Price | Sale Price | Profit |
|------|---------------|-----------|--------------|----------------|------------|--------|
|  |  |  |  |  |  |  |
|  |  |  |  |  |  |  |
|  |  |  |  |  |  |  |
|  |  |  |  |  |  |  |
|  |  |  |  |  |  |  |
|  |  |  |  |  |  |  |
|  |  |  |  |  |  |  |
|  |  |  |  |  |  |  |
|  |  |  |  |  |  |  |
|  |  |  |  |  |  |  |
|  |  |  |  |  |  |  |
|  |  |  |  |  |  |  |
|  |  |  |  |  |  |  |
|  |  |  |  |  |  |  |
|  |  |  |  |  |  |  |
|  |  |  |  |  |  |  |
|  |  |  |  |  |  |  |
|  |  |  |  |  |  |  |
|  |  |  |  |  |  |  |
|  |  |  |  |  |  |  |
|  |  |  |  |  |  |  |
|  |  |  |  |  |  |  |
|  |  |  |  |  |  |  |
|  |  |  |  |  |  |  |
|  |  |  |  |  |  |  |
|  |  |  |  |  |  |  |
|  |  |  |  |  |  |  |

**Total**

# Purchase & Sales Tracker

DATES FROM _____

| Item | Purchase Date | Sale Date | Sale Website | Purchase Price | Sale Price | Profit |
|------|---------------|-----------|--------------|----------------|------------|--------|
|      |               |           |              |                |            |        |
|      |               |           |              |                |            |        |
|      |               |           |              |                |            |        |
|      |               |           |              |                |            |        |
|      |               |           |              |                |            |        |
|      |               |           |              |                |            |        |
|      |               |           |              |                |            |        |
|      |               |           |              |                |            |        |
|      |               |           |              |                |            |        |
|      |               |           |              |                |            |        |
|      |               |           |              |                |            |        |
|      |               |           |              |                |            |        |
|      |               |           |              |                |            |        |
|      |               |           |              |                |            |        |
|      |               |           |              |                |            |        |
|      |               |           |              |                |            |        |
|      |               |           |              |                |            |        |
|      |               |           |              |                |            |        |
|      |               |           |              |                |            |        |
|      |               |           |              |                |            |        |
|      |               |           |              |                |            |        |
|      |               |           |              |                |            |        |
|      |               |           |              |                |            |        |
|      |               |           |              |                |            |        |
|      |               |           |              |                |            |        |
|      |               |           |              |                |            |        |

Total

# Purchase & Sales Tracker

DATES FROM _____

| Item | Purchase Date | Sale Date | Sale Website | Purchase Price | Sale Price | Profit |
|------|---------------|-----------|--------------|----------------|------------|--------|
|  |  |  |  |  |  |  |
|  |  |  |  |  |  |  |
|  |  |  |  |  |  |  |
|  |  |  |  |  |  |  |
|  |  |  |  |  |  |  |
|  |  |  |  |  |  |  |
|  |  |  |  |  |  |  |
|  |  |  |  |  |  |  |
|  |  |  |  |  |  |  |
|  |  |  |  |  |  |  |
|  |  |  |  |  |  |  |
|  |  |  |  |  |  |  |
|  |  |  |  |  |  |  |
|  |  |  |  |  |  |  |
|  |  |  |  |  |  |  |
|  |  |  |  |  |  |  |
|  |  |  |  |  |  |  |
|  |  |  |  |  |  |  |
|  |  |  |  |  |  |  |
|  |  |  |  |  |  |  |
|  |  |  |  |  |  |  |
|  |  |  |  |  |  |  |
|  |  |  |  |  |  |  |
|  |  |  |  |  |  |  |
|  |  |  |  |  |  |  |
|  |  |  |  |  |  |  |
|  |  |  |  |  |  |  |

Total

# Purchase & Sales Tracker

DATES FROM _____

| Item | Purchase Date | Sale Date | Sale Website | Purchase Price | Sale Price | Profit |
|------|---------------|-----------|--------------|----------------|------------|--------|
|      |               |           |              |                |            |        |
|      |               |           |              |                |            |        |
|      |               |           |              |                |            |        |
|      |               |           |              |                |            |        |
|      |               |           |              |                |            |        |
|      |               |           |              |                |            |        |
|      |               |           |              |                |            |        |
|      |               |           |              |                |            |        |
|      |               |           |              |                |            |        |
|      |               |           |              |                |            |        |
|      |               |           |              |                |            |        |
|      |               |           |              |                |            |        |
|      |               |           |              |                |            |        |
|      |               |           |              |                |            |        |
|      |               |           |              |                |            |        |
|      |               |           |              |                |            |        |
|      |               |           |              |                |            |        |
|      |               |           |              |                |            |        |
|      |               |           |              |                |            |        |
|      |               |           |              |                |            |        |
|      |               |           |              |                |            |        |
|      |               |           |              |                |            |        |
|      |               |           |              |                |            |        |
|      |               |           |              |                |            |        |
|      |               |           |              |                |            |        |
|      |               |           |              |                |            |        |
|      |               |           |              |                |            |        |
|      |               |           |              |                |            |        |

**Total**

# Purchase & Sales Tracker

DATES FROM _____

| Item | Purchase Date | Sale Date | Sale Website | Purchase Price | Sale Price | Profit |
|---|---|---|---|---|---|---|
| | | | | | | |
| | | | | | | |
| | | | | | | |
| | | | | | | |
| | | | | | | |
| | | | | | | |
| | | | | | | |
| | | | | | | |
| | | | | | | |
| | | | | | | |
| | | | | | | |
| | | | | | | |
| | | | | | | |
| | | | | | | |
| | | | | | | |
| | | | | | | |
| | | | | | | |
| | | | | | | |
| | | | | | | |
| | | | | | | |
| | | | | | | |
| | | | | | | |
| | | | | | | |
| | | | | | | |
| | | | | | | |
| | | | | | | |
| | | | | | | |

**Total** [        ] [        ] [        ]

# Purchase & Sales Tracker

DATES FROM _____

| Item | Purchase Date | Sale Date | Sale Website | Purchase Price | Sale Price | Profit |
|---|---|---|---|---|---|---|
| | | | | | | |
| | | | | | | |
| | | | | | | |
| | | | | | | |
| | | | | | | |
| | | | | | | |
| | | | | | | |
| | | | | | | |
| | | | | | | |
| | | | | | | |
| | | | | | | |
| | | | | | | |
| | | | | | | |
| | | | | | | |
| | | | | | | |
| | | | | | | |
| | | | | | | |
| | | | | | | |
| | | | | | | |
| | | | | | | |
| | | | | | | |
| | | | | | | |
| | | | | | | |
| | | | | | | |
| | | | | | | |
| | | | | | | |

Total

# Purchase & Sales Tracker

DATES FROM _____

| Item | Purchase Date | Sale Date | Sale Website | Purchase Price | Sale Price | Profit |
|------|---------------|-----------|--------------|----------------|------------|--------|
|      |               |           |              |                |            |        |
|      |               |           |              |                |            |        |
|      |               |           |              |                |            |        |
|      |               |           |              |                |            |        |
|      |               |           |              |                |            |        |
|      |               |           |              |                |            |        |
|      |               |           |              |                |            |        |
|      |               |           |              |                |            |        |
|      |               |           |              |                |            |        |
|      |               |           |              |                |            |        |
|      |               |           |              |                |            |        |
|      |               |           |              |                |            |        |
|      |               |           |              |                |            |        |
|      |               |           |              |                |            |        |
|      |               |           |              |                |            |        |
|      |               |           |              |                |            |        |
|      |               |           |              |                |            |        |
|      |               |           |              |                |            |        |
|      |               |           |              |                |            |        |
|      |               |           |              |                |            |        |
|      |               |           |              |                |            |        |
|      |               |           |              |                |            |        |
|      |               |           |              |                |            |        |
|      |               |           |              |                |            |        |
|      |               |           |              |                |            |        |
|      |               |           |              |                |            |        |
|      |               |           |              |                |            |        |

Total

# Purchase & Sales Tracker

DATES FROM _____

| Item | Purchase Date | Sale Date | Sale Website | Purchase Price | Sale Price | Profit |
|---|---|---|---|---|---|---|
| | | | | | | |
| | | | | | | |
| | | | | | | |
| | | | | | | |
| | | | | | | |
| | | | | | | |
| | | | | | | |
| | | | | | | |
| | | | | | | |
| | | | | | | |
| | | | | | | |
| | | | | | | |
| | | | | | | |
| | | | | | | |
| | | | | | | |
| | | | | | | |
| | | | | | | |
| | | | | | | |
| | | | | | | |
| | | | | | | |
| | | | | | | |
| | | | | | | |
| | | | | | | |
| | | | | | | |
| | | | | | | |
| | | | | | | |
| | | | | | | |
| | | | | | | |

Total

# Purchase & Sales Tracker

DATES FROM _____

| Item | Purchase Date | Sale Date | Sale Website | Purchase Price | Sale Price | Profit |
|------|---------------|-----------|--------------|----------------|------------|--------|
|      |               |           |              |                |            |        |
|      |               |           |              |                |            |        |
|      |               |           |              |                |            |        |
|      |               |           |              |                |            |        |
|      |               |           |              |                |            |        |
|      |               |           |              |                |            |        |
|      |               |           |              |                |            |        |
|      |               |           |              |                |            |        |
|      |               |           |              |                |            |        |
|      |               |           |              |                |            |        |
|      |               |           |              |                |            |        |
|      |               |           |              |                |            |        |
|      |               |           |              |                |            |        |
|      |               |           |              |                |            |        |
|      |               |           |              |                |            |        |
|      |               |           |              |                |            |        |
|      |               |           |              |                |            |        |
|      |               |           |              |                |            |        |
|      |               |           |              |                |            |        |
|      |               |           |              |                |            |        |
|      |               |           |              |                |            |        |
|      |               |           |              |                |            |        |
|      |               |           |              |                |            |        |
|      |               |           |              |                |            |        |
|      |               |           |              |                |            |        |
|      |               |           |              |                |            |        |
|      |               |           |              |                |            |        |
|      |               |           |              |                |            |        |

Total

# Purchase & Sales Tracker

DATES FROM _____

| Item | Purchase Date | Sale Date | Sale Website | Purchase Price | Sale Price | Profit |
|------|---------------|-----------|--------------|----------------|------------|--------|
|      |               |           |              |                |            |        |
|      |               |           |              |                |            |        |
|      |               |           |              |                |            |        |
|      |               |           |              |                |            |        |
|      |               |           |              |                |            |        |
|      |               |           |              |                |            |        |
|      |               |           |              |                |            |        |
|      |               |           |              |                |            |        |
|      |               |           |              |                |            |        |
|      |               |           |              |                |            |        |
|      |               |           |              |                |            |        |
|      |               |           |              |                |            |        |
|      |               |           |              |                |            |        |
|      |               |           |              |                |            |        |
|      |               |           |              |                |            |        |
|      |               |           |              |                |            |        |
|      |               |           |              |                |            |        |
|      |               |           |              |                |            |        |
|      |               |           |              |                |            |        |
|      |               |           |              |                |            |        |
|      |               |           |              |                |            |        |
|      |               |           |              |                |            |        |
|      |               |           |              |                |            |        |
|      |               |           |              |                |            |        |
|      |               |           |              |                |            |        |
|      |               |           |              |                |            |        |
|      |               |           |              |                |            |        |

Total

# Purchase & Sales Tracker

DATES FROM _____

| Item | Purchase Date | Sale Date | Sale Website | Purchase Price | Sale Price | Profit |
|---|---|---|---|---|---|---|
|  |  |  |  |  |  |  |
|  |  |  |  |  |  |  |
|  |  |  |  |  |  |  |
|  |  |  |  |  |  |  |
|  |  |  |  |  |  |  |
|  |  |  |  |  |  |  |
|  |  |  |  |  |  |  |
|  |  |  |  |  |  |  |
|  |  |  |  |  |  |  |
|  |  |  |  |  |  |  |
|  |  |  |  |  |  |  |
|  |  |  |  |  |  |  |
|  |  |  |  |  |  |  |
|  |  |  |  |  |  |  |
|  |  |  |  |  |  |  |
|  |  |  |  |  |  |  |
|  |  |  |  |  |  |  |
|  |  |  |  |  |  |  |
|  |  |  |  |  |  |  |
|  |  |  |  |  |  |  |
|  |  |  |  |  |  |  |
|  |  |  |  |  |  |  |
|  |  |  |  |  |  |  |
|  |  |  |  |  |  |  |
|  |  |  |  |  |  |  |
|  |  |  |  |  |  |  |
|  |  |  |  |  |  |  |
|  |  |  |  |  |  |  |
|  |  |  |  |  |  |  |

Total

# Purchase & Sales Tracker

DATES FROM _____

| Item | Purchase Date | Sale Date | Sale Website | Purchase Price | Sale Price | Profit |
|------|---------------|-----------|--------------|----------------|------------|--------|
|      |               |           |              |                |            |        |
|      |               |           |              |                |            |        |
|      |               |           |              |                |            |        |
|      |               |           |              |                |            |        |
|      |               |           |              |                |            |        |
|      |               |           |              |                |            |        |
|      |               |           |              |                |            |        |
|      |               |           |              |                |            |        |
|      |               |           |              |                |            |        |
|      |               |           |              |                |            |        |
|      |               |           |              |                |            |        |
|      |               |           |              |                |            |        |
|      |               |           |              |                |            |        |
|      |               |           |              |                |            |        |
|      |               |           |              |                |            |        |
|      |               |           |              |                |            |        |
|      |               |           |              |                |            |        |
|      |               |           |              |                |            |        |
|      |               |           |              |                |            |        |
|      |               |           |              |                |            |        |
|      |               |           |              |                |            |        |
|      |               |           |              |                |            |        |
|      |               |           |              |                |            |        |
|      |               |           |              |                |            |        |
|      |               |           |              |                |            |        |
|      |               |           |              |                |            |        |
|      |               |           |              |                |            |        |

Total

# Purchase & Sales Tracker

DATES FROM _____

| Item | Purchase Date | Sale Date | Sale Website | Purchase Price | Sale Price | Profit |
|------|------|------|------|------|------|------|
|  |  |  |  |  |  |  |
|  |  |  |  |  |  |  |
|  |  |  |  |  |  |  |
|  |  |  |  |  |  |  |
|  |  |  |  |  |  |  |
|  |  |  |  |  |  |  |
|  |  |  |  |  |  |  |
|  |  |  |  |  |  |  |
|  |  |  |  |  |  |  |
|  |  |  |  |  |  |  |
|  |  |  |  |  |  |  |
|  |  |  |  |  |  |  |
|  |  |  |  |  |  |  |
|  |  |  |  |  |  |  |
|  |  |  |  |  |  |  |
|  |  |  |  |  |  |  |
|  |  |  |  |  |  |  |
|  |  |  |  |  |  |  |
|  |  |  |  |  |  |  |
|  |  |  |  |  |  |  |
|  |  |  |  |  |  |  |
|  |  |  |  |  |  |  |
|  |  |  |  |  |  |  |
|  |  |  |  |  |  |  |
|  |  |  |  |  |  |  |
|  |  |  |  |  |  |  |
|  |  |  |  |  |  |  |
|  |  |  |  |  |  |  |
|  |  |  |  |  |  |  |

Total

# Purchase & Sales Tracker

DATES FROM _____

| Item | Purchase Date | Sale Date | Sale Website | Purchase Price | Sale Price | Profit |
|------|---------------|-----------|--------------|----------------|------------|--------|
|      |               |           |              |                |            |        |
|      |               |           |              |                |            |        |
|      |               |           |              |                |            |        |
|      |               |           |              |                |            |        |
|      |               |           |              |                |            |        |
|      |               |           |              |                |            |        |
|      |               |           |              |                |            |        |
|      |               |           |              |                |            |        |
|      |               |           |              |                |            |        |
|      |               |           |              |                |            |        |
|      |               |           |              |                |            |        |
|      |               |           |              |                |            |        |
|      |               |           |              |                |            |        |
|      |               |           |              |                |            |        |
|      |               |           |              |                |            |        |
|      |               |           |              |                |            |        |
|      |               |           |              |                |            |        |
|      |               |           |              |                |            |        |
|      |               |           |              |                |            |        |
|      |               |           |              |                |            |        |
|      |               |           |              |                |            |        |
|      |               |           |              |                |            |        |
|      |               |           |              |                |            |        |
|      |               |           |              |                |            |        |
|      |               |           |              |                |            |        |
|      |               |           |              |                |            |        |
|      |               |           |              |                |            |        |

Total

# Purchase & Sales Tracker

DATES FROM _____

| Item | Purchase Date | Sale Date | Sale Website | Purchase Price | Sale Price | Profit |
|------|---------------|-----------|--------------|----------------|------------|--------|
| | | | | | | |
| | | | | | | |
| | | | | | | |
| | | | | | | |
| | | | | | | |
| | | | | | | |
| | | | | | | |
| | | | | | | |
| | | | | | | |
| | | | | | | |
| | | | | | | |
| | | | | | | |
| | | | | | | |
| | | | | | | |
| | | | | | | |
| | | | | | | |
| | | | | | | |
| | | | | | | |
| | | | | | | |
| | | | | | | |
| | | | | | | |
| | | | | | | |
| | | | | | | |
| | | | | | | |
| | | | | | | |
| | | | | | | |
| | | | | | | |

**Total** | | |

# Purchase & Sales Tracker

DATES FROM _____

| Item | Purchase Date | Sale Date | Sale Website | Purchase Price | Sale Price | Profit |
|------|---------------|-----------|--------------|----------------|------------|--------|
|  |  |  |  |  |  |  |
|  |  |  |  |  |  |  |
|  |  |  |  |  |  |  |
|  |  |  |  |  |  |  |
|  |  |  |  |  |  |  |
|  |  |  |  |  |  |  |
|  |  |  |  |  |  |  |
|  |  |  |  |  |  |  |
|  |  |  |  |  |  |  |
|  |  |  |  |  |  |  |
|  |  |  |  |  |  |  |
|  |  |  |  |  |  |  |
|  |  |  |  |  |  |  |
|  |  |  |  |  |  |  |
|  |  |  |  |  |  |  |
|  |  |  |  |  |  |  |
|  |  |  |  |  |  |  |
|  |  |  |  |  |  |  |
|  |  |  |  |  |  |  |
|  |  |  |  |  |  |  |
|  |  |  |  |  |  |  |
|  |  |  |  |  |  |  |
|  |  |  |  |  |  |  |
|  |  |  |  |  |  |  |
|  |  |  |  |  |  |  |
|  |  |  |  |  |  |  |
|  |  |  |  |  |  |  |

Total

# Purchase & Sales Tracker

DATES FROM _____

| Item | Purchase Date | Sale Date | Sale Website | Purchase Price | Sale Price | Profit |
|------|--------------|-----------|--------------|----------------|------------|--------|
|      |              |           |              |                |            |        |
|      |              |           |              |                |            |        |
|      |              |           |              |                |            |        |
|      |              |           |              |                |            |        |
|      |              |           |              |                |            |        |
|      |              |           |              |                |            |        |
|      |              |           |              |                |            |        |
|      |              |           |              |                |            |        |
|      |              |           |              |                |            |        |
|      |              |           |              |                |            |        |
|      |              |           |              |                |            |        |
|      |              |           |              |                |            |        |
|      |              |           |              |                |            |        |
|      |              |           |              |                |            |        |
|      |              |           |              |                |            |        |
|      |              |           |              |                |            |        |
|      |              |           |              |                |            |        |
|      |              |           |              |                |            |        |
|      |              |           |              |                |            |        |
|      |              |           |              |                |            |        |
|      |              |           |              |                |            |        |
|      |              |           |              |                |            |        |
|      |              |           |              |                |            |        |
|      |              |           |              |                |            |        |
|      |              |           |              |                |            |        |
|      |              |           |              |                |            |        |

Total

# Purchase & Sales Tracker

DATES FROM _____

| Item | Purchase Date | Sale Date | Sale Website | Purchase Price | Sale Price | Profit |
|------|---------------|-----------|--------------|----------------|------------|--------|
|      |               |           |              |                |            |        |
|      |               |           |              |                |            |        |
|      |               |           |              |                |            |        |
|      |               |           |              |                |            |        |
|      |               |           |              |                |            |        |
|      |               |           |              |                |            |        |
|      |               |           |              |                |            |        |
|      |               |           |              |                |            |        |
|      |               |           |              |                |            |        |
|      |               |           |              |                |            |        |
|      |               |           |              |                |            |        |
|      |               |           |              |                |            |        |
|      |               |           |              |                |            |        |
|      |               |           |              |                |            |        |
|      |               |           |              |                |            |        |
|      |               |           |              |                |            |        |
|      |               |           |              |                |            |        |
|      |               |           |              |                |            |        |
|      |               |           |              |                |            |        |
|      |               |           |              |                |            |        |
|      |               |           |              |                |            |        |
|      |               |           |              |                |            |        |
|      |               |           |              |                |            |        |
|      |               |           |              |                |            |        |
|      |               |           |              |                |            |        |
|      |               |           |              |                |            |        |
|      |               |           |              |                |            |        |
|      |               |           |              |                |            |        |

Total

# Purchase & Sales Tracker

DATES FROM _____

| Item | Purchase Date | Sale Date | Sale Website | Purchase Price | Sale Price | Profit |
|------|---------------|-----------|--------------|----------------|------------|--------|
|      |               |           |              |                |            |        |
|      |               |           |              |                |            |        |
|      |               |           |              |                |            |        |
|      |               |           |              |                |            |        |
|      |               |           |              |                |            |        |
|      |               |           |              |                |            |        |
|      |               |           |              |                |            |        |
|      |               |           |              |                |            |        |
|      |               |           |              |                |            |        |
|      |               |           |              |                |            |        |
|      |               |           |              |                |            |        |
|      |               |           |              |                |            |        |
|      |               |           |              |                |            |        |
|      |               |           |              |                |            |        |
|      |               |           |              |                |            |        |
|      |               |           |              |                |            |        |
|      |               |           |              |                |            |        |
|      |               |           |              |                |            |        |
|      |               |           |              |                |            |        |
|      |               |           |              |                |            |        |
|      |               |           |              |                |            |        |
|      |               |           |              |                |            |        |
|      |               |           |              |                |            |        |
|      |               |           |              |                |            |        |
|      |               |           |              |                |            |        |
|      |               |           |              |                |            |        |

Total

# Purchase & Sales Tracker

DATES FROM _____

| Item | Purchase Date | Sale Date | Sale Website | Purchase Price | Sale Price | Profit |
|------|---------------|-----------|--------------|----------------|------------|--------|
|  |  |  |  |  |  |  |
|  |  |  |  |  |  |  |
|  |  |  |  |  |  |  |
|  |  |  |  |  |  |  |
|  |  |  |  |  |  |  |
|  |  |  |  |  |  |  |
|  |  |  |  |  |  |  |
|  |  |  |  |  |  |  |
|  |  |  |  |  |  |  |
|  |  |  |  |  |  |  |
|  |  |  |  |  |  |  |
|  |  |  |  |  |  |  |
|  |  |  |  |  |  |  |
|  |  |  |  |  |  |  |
|  |  |  |  |  |  |  |
|  |  |  |  |  |  |  |
|  |  |  |  |  |  |  |
|  |  |  |  |  |  |  |
|  |  |  |  |  |  |  |
|  |  |  |  |  |  |  |
|  |  |  |  |  |  |  |
|  |  |  |  |  |  |  |
|  |  |  |  |  |  |  |
|  |  |  |  |  |  |  |
|  |  |  |  |  |  |  |
|  |  |  |  |  |  |  |

Total

# Purchase & Sales Tracker

DATES FROM _____

| Item | Purchase Date | Sale Date | Sale Website | Purchase Price | Sale Price | Profit |
|------|---------------|-----------|--------------|----------------|------------|--------|
|  |  |  |  |  |  |  |
|  |  |  |  |  |  |  |
|  |  |  |  |  |  |  |
|  |  |  |  |  |  |  |
|  |  |  |  |  |  |  |
|  |  |  |  |  |  |  |
|  |  |  |  |  |  |  |
|  |  |  |  |  |  |  |
|  |  |  |  |  |  |  |
|  |  |  |  |  |  |  |
|  |  |  |  |  |  |  |
|  |  |  |  |  |  |  |
|  |  |  |  |  |  |  |
|  |  |  |  |  |  |  |
|  |  |  |  |  |  |  |
|  |  |  |  |  |  |  |
|  |  |  |  |  |  |  |
|  |  |  |  |  |  |  |
|  |  |  |  |  |  |  |
|  |  |  |  |  |  |  |
|  |  |  |  |  |  |  |
|  |  |  |  |  |  |  |
|  |  |  |  |  |  |  |
|  |  |  |  |  |  |  |
|  |  |  |  |  |  |  |

Total

# Purchase & Sales Tracker

DATES FROM _____

| Item | Purchase Date | Sale Date | Sale Website | Purchase Price | Sale Price | Profit |
|------|---------------|-----------|--------------|----------------|------------|--------|
|  |  |  |  |  |  |  |
|  |  |  |  |  |  |  |
|  |  |  |  |  |  |  |
|  |  |  |  |  |  |  |
|  |  |  |  |  |  |  |
|  |  |  |  |  |  |  |
|  |  |  |  |  |  |  |
|  |  |  |  |  |  |  |
|  |  |  |  |  |  |  |
|  |  |  |  |  |  |  |
|  |  |  |  |  |  |  |
|  |  |  |  |  |  |  |
|  |  |  |  |  |  |  |
|  |  |  |  |  |  |  |
|  |  |  |  |  |  |  |
|  |  |  |  |  |  |  |
|  |  |  |  |  |  |  |
|  |  |  |  |  |  |  |
|  |  |  |  |  |  |  |
|  |  |  |  |  |  |  |
|  |  |  |  |  |  |  |
|  |  |  |  |  |  |  |
|  |  |  |  |  |  |  |
|  |  |  |  |  |  |  |
|  |  |  |  |  |  |  |
|  |  |  |  |  |  |  |
|  |  |  |  |  |  |  |

Total

# Purchase & Sales Tracker

DATES FROM _____

| Item | Purchase Date | Sale Date | Sale Website | Purchase Price | Sale Price | Profit |
|---|---|---|---|---|---|---|
|  |  |  |  |  |  |  |
|  |  |  |  |  |  |  |
|  |  |  |  |  |  |  |
|  |  |  |  |  |  |  |
|  |  |  |  |  |  |  |
|  |  |  |  |  |  |  |
|  |  |  |  |  |  |  |
|  |  |  |  |  |  |  |
|  |  |  |  |  |  |  |
|  |  |  |  |  |  |  |
|  |  |  |  |  |  |  |
|  |  |  |  |  |  |  |
|  |  |  |  |  |  |  |
|  |  |  |  |  |  |  |
|  |  |  |  |  |  |  |
|  |  |  |  |  |  |  |
|  |  |  |  |  |  |  |
|  |  |  |  |  |  |  |
|  |  |  |  |  |  |  |
|  |  |  |  |  |  |  |
|  |  |  |  |  |  |  |
|  |  |  |  |  |  |  |
|  |  |  |  |  |  |  |
|  |  |  |  |  |  |  |
|  |  |  |  |  |  |  |
|  |  |  |  |  |  |  |
|  |  |  |  |  |  |  |
|  |  |  |  |  |  |  |
|  |  |  |  |  |  |  |

Total

# Purchase & Sales Tracker

DATES FROM _____

| Item | Purchase Date | Sale Date | Sale Website | Purchase Price | Sale Price | Profit |
|------|---------------|-----------|--------------|----------------|------------|--------|
| | | | | | | |
| | | | | | | |
| | | | | | | |
| | | | | | | |
| | | | | | | |
| | | | | | | |
| | | | | | | |
| | | | | | | |
| | | | | | | |
| | | | | | | |
| | | | | | | |
| | | | | | | |
| | | | | | | |
| | | | | | | |
| | | | | | | |
| | | | | | | |
| | | | | | | |
| | | | | | | |
| | | | | | | |
| | | | | | | |
| | | | | | | |
| | | | | | | |
| | | | | | | |
| | | | | | | |
| | | | | | | |
| | | | | | | |

Total

# Purchase & Sales Tracker

DATES FROM _____

| Item | Purchase Date | Sale Date | Sale Website | Purchase Price | Sale Price | Profit |
|---|---|---|---|---|---|---|
| | | | | | | |
| | | | | | | |
| | | | | | | |
| | | | | | | |
| | | | | | | |
| | | | | | | |
| | | | | | | |
| | | | | | | |
| | | | | | | |
| | | | | | | |
| | | | | | | |
| | | | | | | |
| | | | | | | |
| | | | | | | |
| | | | | | | |
| | | | | | | |
| | | | | | | |
| | | | | | | |
| | | | | | | |
| | | | | | | |
| | | | | | | |
| | | | | | | |
| | | | | | | |
| | | | | | | |
| | | | | | | |
| | | | | | | |
| | | | | | | |
| | | | | | | |

Total

# Purchase & Sales Tracker

| Item | Purchase Date | Sale Date | Sale Website | Purchase Price | Sale Price | Profit |
|------|---------------|-----------|--------------|----------------|------------|--------|
|      |               |           |              |                |            |        |
|      |               |           |              |                |            |        |
|      |               |           |              |                |            |        |
|      |               |           |              |                |            |        |
|      |               |           |              |                |            |        |
|      |               |           |              |                |            |        |
|      |               |           |              |                |            |        |
|      |               |           |              |                |            |        |
|      |               |           |              |                |            |        |
|      |               |           |              |                |            |        |
|      |               |           |              |                |            |        |
|      |               |           |              |                |            |        |
|      |               |           |              |                |            |        |
|      |               |           |              |                |            |        |
|      |               |           |              |                |            |        |
|      |               |           |              |                |            |        |
|      |               |           |              |                |            |        |
|      |               |           |              |                |            |        |
|      |               |           |              |                |            |        |
|      |               |           |              |                |            |        |
|      |               |           |              |                |            |        |
|      |               |           |              |                |            |        |
|      |               |           |              |                |            |        |
|      |               |           |              |                |            |        |
|      |               |           |              |                |            |        |
|      |               |           |              |                |            |        |
|      |               |           |              |                |            |        |
|      |               |           |              |                |            |        |

Total

www.ingramcontent.com/pod-product-compliance
Lightning Source LLC
Chambersburg PA
CBHW081010170526
45158CB00010B/2987